SpringerBriefs in Rights-Based Approaches to Social Work

Series Editor
Shirley Gatenio Gabel, New York, NY, USA

SpringerBriefs present concise summaries of cutting-edge research and practical applications. Featuring compact volumes of 50 to 125 pages, the series covers a range of content from professional to academic. Typical topics might include:

- A timely report of state-of-the art analytical techniques
- A bridge between new research results, as published in journal articles, and a contextual literature review
- A snapshot of a hot or emerging topic
- An in-depth case study or clinical example
- A presentation of core concepts that students must understand in order to make independent contributions

SpringerBriefs in Human Rights and Social Work Practice explore the applicability of a human rights framework to social policy analysis, international social development, advocacy, and research. Briefs are characterized by fast, global electronic dissemination and expedited production schedules.

More information about this series at http://www.springer.com/series/11694

Karen Rice • Heather Girvin

Human Rights-Based Approach to Short-Term Study Abroad

Springer

Karen Rice
School of Social Work
Millersville University
Millersville, PA, USA

Heather Girvin
School of Social Work
Millersville University
Millersville, PA, USA

ISSN 2195-9749 ISSN 2195-9757 (electronic)
SpringerBriefs in Rights-Based Approaches to Social Work
ISBN 978-3-030-87420-9 ISBN 978-3-030-87421-6 (eBook)
https://doi.org/10.1007/978-3-030-87421-6

This Springer imprint is published by the registered company Springer Nature Switzerland AG
The registered company address is: Gewerbestrasse 11, 6330 Cham, Switzerland

To all the members of the host communities we have visited, thank you for your exceptional hospitality, grace, and patience. The connections we made that turned into lasting friendships have been the greatest gifts!

For Austin, Karlee, and Heather, who remind me daily of the importance of creating a more just world. — Karen Rice

For Wyatt, Agnes, and Adeline, who broaden my view and inspire my dedication to social justice. — Heather Girvin

Foreword

Even though you and I are in different boats, you in your boat and we in our canoe, we share the same River of Life.
—Chief Oren Lyons, Onandaga Nation, USA

The rights of every man are diminished when the rights of one man are threatened.
—John F. Kennedy, Civil Rights Announcement, June 11, 1963

For over a century, social workers have worked to improve the lives and situations of individuals, families, and communities. Social workers, often acting on behalf of the state's interests, typically intervened according to what they themselves perceived to be deficits in the lives and behaviors of persons in need. This approach to working with people patronizes, stigmatizes, and too often revictimizes those we seek to assist. It is long past time to revitalize and reframe our approach to working with those we seek to serve. The books in this series reframe deficit models used by social work practitioners and instead propose a human rights perspective. Rights-based social work shifts the focus from human needs to human rights and calls on social workers and the populations they work with to actively participate in decision-making processes of the state so that the state can better serve the interests of the population. The authors in the series share their strategies for empowering the populations and individuals we, as social workers, engage with as clinicians, community workers, researchers, and policy analysts.

The roots of social work in the United States can be traced to the pioneering efforts of upper-class men and women who established church-based and secular charitable organizations that sought to address the consequences of poverty, urbanization, and immigration. These were issues that were ignored by the public sphere at the time. Little in the way of training or methods was offered to those who volunteered their resources, efforts, and time in these charitable organizations until later in the nineteenth century when concepts derived from business and industry were applied to distribution of relief efforts in what became known as "scientific charity." This scientific approach led to the use of investigation, registration, and supervision of applicants for charity, and in 1877, the first American Charity Organization Society (COS) was founded in Buffalo, New York. The popularity of the approach grew quickly across the country. COS leaders wanted to reform charity by including an agent's investigation of the case's "worthiness" before distributing aid because they believed that unregulated and unsupervised relief led to more calls for relief.

Around the same time, an alternative response to the impact of industrialization and immigration was introduced and tested by the settlement house movement. The first US settlement, the Neighborhood Guild in New York City, was established in 1886, and less than 3 years later, Jane Addams and Ellen Gates Starr founded Hull House in Chicago, which came to symbolize the settlement house movement in the United States. Unlike the individually oriented COS, the settlement house movement focused on the environmental causes of poverty, seeking economic and social reforms for the poor and providing largely immigrant and migrant populations with the skills needed to stake their claims in American society.

The settlement house movement spread rapidly in the United States, and by 1910, there were more than 400 settlements (Friedman and Friedman, 2006; Trolander, 1987). Advocacy for rights and social justice became an important component of the settlement activities and led to the creation of national organizations like the National Consumers' League, Urban League, Women's Trade Union League, and the National Association for the Advancement of Colored People (NAACP). The leaders of the movement led major social movements of the period, including women's suffrage, peace, labor, civil rights, and temperance, and were instrumental in establishing a federal-level children's bureau in 1912, headed by Julia Lathrop from Hull House.

During this same period, the charity organization societies set to standardize the casework skills for their work with individuals. Their methods became a distinct area of practice and were formalized as a social work training program in 1898 known as the New York School of Philanthropy, and eventually the Columbia University School of Social Work. In 1908, the Chicago Commons offered a full curriculum through the Chicago School of Civics and Philanthropy (now the University of Chicago's School of Social Service Administration) based on the practices and principles of the settlement movement. By 1919, there were 17 schools of social work.

Efforts already underway to secure and strengthen pragmatically derived casework knowledge into a standardized format were accelerated following Abraham Flexner's provocative lecture in 1915 questioning whether social work was a profession because he believed it lacked specificity, technical skills, or specialized knowledge (Morris, 2008). By the 1920s, casework emerged as the dominant form of professional social work in the United States and remained primarily focused on aiding impoverished children and families but was rapidly expanding to work with veterans and middle-class individuals in child-guidance clinics.

As social work branched out to other populations, it increasingly focused on refining clinical treatment modalities, and over time, clinical work too often stood apart from community work, advocacy, and social policy. Although social work education standards today require all students to be exposed to clinical and casework, community practice, advocacy, research, and policy, most schools do not prioritize the integrated practice of these areas in the advanced year of social work education (Austin and Ezell, 2004; Knee and Folsom, 2012).

Despite the development of sophisticated methods for helping others, social work practice overly relies on charity and needs-based approaches. These approaches are built on the deficit model of practice in which professionals or individuals with greater means diagnose what is "needed" in a situation and the "treatment" or services required to yield the desired outcome that has been set by the profession or other persons of advantage. Judgments of need are based on professional research, practice wisdom, and theory steeped in values (Ife, 2012). These values, research, theories, and practices typically reflect the beliefs of the persons pronouncing judgment, not necessarily the values and theories of the person who is being judged. This has the effect of disempowering and diminishing control of one's own life while privileging professionals (Ife, 2012). In turn, this risks reinforcing passiveness and perpetuating the violation of rights among the marginalized populations we seek to empower and at best maintains the status quo in society.

Needs-based approaches typically arise from charitable intentions. In social welfare, charity-based efforts have led to the labeling of persons worthy and unworthy of assistance, attributing personal behaviors as the cause of marginalization, poverty, disease, and disenfranchisement, and restricted the types of aid available accordingly. Judgments are cast by elites regarding who is deserving and who is not based on criteria that serve to perpetuate existing social, economic, and political relationships in charity-based approaches. Needs-based approaches attempt to introduce greater objectivity into the process of selecting who is helped and how by using evidence to demonstrate need and introducing effective and efficient interventions to improve the lot of the needy and society as a whole. Yet the solutions of needs-based efforts like charity-based ones are laden with the values of professionals and the politically elite and do not necessarily reflect the values and choices of the persons who are the object of assistance. Needs-based approaches prioritize the achievement of professionally established goals over the process of developing the goals, and, too often, the failure of outcomes is attributed to personal attributes or behaviors of individuals or groups who receive assistance. For example, the type of services a person diagnosed with a mental disorder receives in a needs-based approach will be often decided by authorities or experts according to their determination of what is best for the person and is likely to assume that a person with a mental disorder is incapable of making choices or at least not "good" choices. Programmatic success would then be evaluated according to adherence to the treatment plan prescribed by the persons with authority in the situation and may omit consumers' objections or own assessments of well-being.

Unlike needs-based and charity-based approaches, a rights-based approach places equal value on process and outcome. In rights-based work, goals are temporary markers that are adjusted as people perpetually re-evaluate and understand rights in new ways calling for new approaches to social issues. For example, having nearly achieved universal access to primary education, a re-evaluation of the right to education might lead to a new goal to raise the quality of education or promote universal enrollment in secondary education among girls. Rights-based approaches are anchored in a normative framework that are based in a set of internationally agreed upon legal covenants and conventions, which in and of themselves can provide a different and potentially more powerful approach. A key aspect of this approach posits the right of all persons to participate in societal decision-making, especially those persons or groups that are affected by the decisions. For example, Article 12 of the United Nations Convention on the Rights of the Child (UNCRC) asserts that states "shall assure to the child who is capable of forming his or her own views the right to express those views freely in all matters affecting the child, the views of the child being given due weight in accordance with the age and maturity of the child" (UNCRC, 1989). Likewise, the preamble to the United Nations Convention on the Rights of Persons with Disabilities (UNCRPD) holds states responsible for "redressing the profound social disadvantage of persons with disabilities and (to) promote their participation in the civil, political, economic, social, and cultural spheres with equal opportunities" (UNCRPD, 2006).

A rights-based approach requires consideration of the universally recognized principles of human rights: the equality of each individual as a human being, the inherent dignity of each person, and the rights to self-determination, peace, and security. Respect for all human rights sets the foundation for all civil, political, social, and economic goals that seek to establish certain standards of well-being for all persons. Rights-based efforts remove the charity dimension by recognizing people not only as beneficiaries, but as active rights holders.

One of the areas of value added by the human rights approach is the emphasis it places on the *accountability* of policy makers and other actors whose actions have an impact on the rights of people. Unlike needs, rights imply duties, and duties demand accountability (UN OHCHR, 2002: paragraph 23). Whereas needs may be met or satisfied, rights are realized and as such must be respected, protected, facilitated, and fulfilled. Human rights are indivisible and interdependent, and unlike needs that can be ranked, all human rights are of equal importance. A central dynamic of a rights-based approach is thus about identifying root causes of social issues and empowering rights holders to understand and if possible claim their rights while duty bearers are enabled to meet their obligations. Under international law, the state is the principal duty bearer with respect to the human rights of the people living within its jurisdiction. However, the international community at large also has a responsibility to help realize universal human rights. Thus, monitoring and accountability procedures extend beyond states to global actors—such as the donor community, intergovernmental organizations, international non-governmental organizations (NGOs), and transnational corporations—whose actions bear upon the enjoyment of human rights in any country (UN OHCHR, 2002: paragraph 230).

Table 1 summarizes the differences between charity-, needs-, and rights-based approaches.

It can be argued that rights-based practice is not strikingly different from the way many social workers practice. For example, the strengths perspective that has become a popular approach in social work practice since the 1990s focuses on strengths, abilities, and potential rather than problems, deficits, and pathologies (Chapin, 1995; Early & GlenMaye, 2000; Saleebey, 1992a) and "interventions are

Table 1 Comparison of charity-, needs-, and rights-based approaches to social issues

	Charity-based	Needs-based	Rights-based
Goals	Assistance to deserving and disadvantaged individuals or populations to relieve immediate suffering	Fulfilling an identified deficit in individuals or community through additional resources for marginalized and disadvantaged groups	Realization of human rights that will lead to the equitable allocation of resources and power
Motivation	Religious or moral imperative of rich or endowed to help the less fortunate who are deserving of assistance	To help those deemed in need of help so as to promote well-being of societal members	Legal obligation to entitlements
Accountability	May be accountable to private organization	Generally accountable to those who identified the need and developed the intervention	Governments and global bodies such as the donor community, intergovernmental organizations, international NGOs, and transnational corporations
Process	Philanthropic with emphasis on donor	Expert identification of need, its dimensions, and strategy for meeting need within political negotiation. Affected population is the object of interventions	Political with a focus on participatory process in which individuals and groups are empowered to claim their rights
Power relationships	Preserves status quo	Largely maintain existing structure, change might be incremental	Must change
Target population of efforts	Individuals and populations worthy of assistance	Disadvantaged individuals or populations	All members of society with an emphasis on marginalized populations
Emphasis	On donor's benevolent actions	On meeting needs	On the realization of human rights
Interventions respond to	Immediate manifestation of problems	Symptomatic deficits and may address structural causes	Fundamental structural causes while providing alleviation from symptomatic manifestations

directed to the uniqueness, skills, interests, hopes, and desires of each consumer, rather than a categorical litany of deficits" (Kisthardt, 1992: 60–61). In the strengths-based approach, clients are usually seen as the experts on their own situation and professionals are understood as not necessarily having the "best vantage point from which to appreciate client strengths" (Saleebey, 1992b, p. 7). The focus is on "collaboration and partnership between social workers and clients" (Early & GlenMaye, 2000: 120).

The strengths perspective has provided a way for many social workers to engage themselves and the populations they work with in advocacy and empowerment that builds upon capabilities and more active processes of social change. Indeed, strengths-based and rights-based approaches build upon the strengths of individuals and communities and both involve a shift from a deficit approach to one that reinforces the potential of individuals and communities. Both approaches acknowledge the unique sets of strengths and challenges of individuals and communities and engage them as partners in developing and implementing interventions to improve well-being giving consideration to the complexities of environments. However, the strengths-based perspective falls short of empowering individuals to claim their rights within a universal, normative framework that goes beyond social work to cut across every professional discipline and applies to all human beings. Rights-based approaches tie social work practice into a global strategy that asserts universal entitlements as well as the accountability of governments and other actors who bear responsibility for furthering the realization of human rights.

The link between social work and human rights normative standards is an important one as history has repeatedly demonstrated. In many ways, social work has been moving toward these standards (Healy, 2008) but has yet to fully embrace it. Social work has been a contradictory and perplexing profession functioning both to help and also to control the disadvantaged. At times social workers have engaged in roles that have furthered oppression (Ife, 2012) and served as a "handmaiden" to those who seek to preserve the status quo (Abramovitz, 1998, p. 512). Social benefits can be used to integrate marginalized populations but also be used to privilege and exclude, particularly when a charity-based approach is utilized. When conditional, benefits can also be used as a way to modify behaviors and as a means of collecting information on private individual and family matters.

This contradictory and perplexing role of social work is shown albeit, in an extreme case, by social work involvement in the social eugenics movement specifically promulgated by National Socialists leaders in the 1930s and 1940s (Johnson & Moorehead, 2011). Leading up to and during World War II, social workers were used as instruments to implement Nazi policies in Europe. Though the history of social work and social work education is different in each European country, in at least Germany, Austria, Switzerland, Czechoslovakia, and Hungary, authorities used social workers to exclude what the state considered at the time to be undesirable populations from assistance, to reward those who demonstrated loyalty and pledged to carry forth the ideology of the state, and to collect information on personal and family affairs for the state (Hauss & Schulte, 2009). University-based and other forms of social work training were closed down in Germany in 1933 when the National Socialists assumed control because welfare was regarded as superfluous and a "waste for persons useless to the national community" (*Volksgemeinschaft* as quoted in Hauss & Schulte, 2009, p. 9). "Inferiors" were denied support and social workers were re-educated in Nazi ideology to train mothers on how to raise children who were loyal and useful to the ambitions of the National Socialists (Kruse, 2009). Similarly in Hungary, where social workers were referred to as "social sisters," social workers were re-educated to train mothers about the value of their contributions to the state (mainly their reproductive capacity and rearing of strong children for the state) and were instrumental in the implementation of Hungary's major welfare program that rewarded "worthy" clients with the redistribution of assets from Jewish estates (Szikra, 2009). As Szrika notes, "In the 1930s social policy and social work constituted a central part of social and economic policy-making that was fueled by nationalist and anti-Semitic ideology, influenced by similar practices in Germany, Italy and Czechoslavakia" (p. 116). Following Nazi ideological inoculation based on eugenics and race hate, social workers in Austria were charged with the responsibility of collecting incriminating information regarding mental illness, venereal disease, prostitution, alcoholism, hereditary diseases, and disabilities that would then be used to deny social benefits, prohibit marriages, and even select children for Austria's euthanasia program (Melinz, 2009).

Using social workers to realize state ideology was also employed to advance the Soviet agenda beginning in 1918 (Iarskaia-Smirnova & Romanov, 2009). The provision of social services was distributed across multiple disciplines among the helping professions and the term social work was not used because of its association to Western social welfare (Iarskaia-Smirnova & Romanov, 2009). These professionals, often referred to as social agents (workers in nurseries and youth centers, activists in women's organizations and trade unions, nurses, educators, and domestic affairs officials), were charged with the double task of social care and control. Early on social agents contributed to the establishment of standards designating worthy and unworthy behavior and activities and practices such as censure and social exclusion designed to alienate those who did not comply with state goals (Iarskaia-Smirnova & Romanov, 2009).

The use of social workers to carry out goals seemingly in contradiction of social work's ethics can be found in many examples in the United States as well (Abramovitz, 1998). In his book, *The Child Savers: The Invention of Delinquency* (1965), Anthony Platt demonstrates that despite well-intentioned efforts to protect youth, the establishment of the juvenile justice system in the United States removed youth from the adult justice systems and in doing so created a class of delinquents who were judged without due process. Platt argues that "child savers should in no sense be considered libertarians or humanists" (Platt, 1965, p. 176). The juvenile justice system that these reformers—many of whom were social work pioneers—created in the United States purposefully blurred the distinction between delinquent and dependent young people. Labeling dependent children as delinquents, most of whom had committed no crime, robbed them of their opportunity to due process. The state and various religious organizations were given open reign to define delinquency as they saw fit and children who were perceived to be out of order or young women who were viewed as immoral were committed to institutions or other forms of state supervision with no means of redress.

More recently, Bumiller's analysis of domestic violence in the United States rouses our consciousness of the ways in which social workers engaged with persons involved in domestic violence and/or rape may inadvertently squash rather than empower individuals and families (Bumiller, 2008). Bumiller (2008) uses sexual violence to demonstrate how lawyers, medical professionals, and social workers may be contributing to passivity of social service beneficiaries and in doing so, enlarge the state's ability to control the behaviors of its members. As Bumiller explains, our public branding of perpetrators of sexual violence as deserving of severe punishment and isolation allow us then to deem them incapable of rehabilitation, and so we offer few opportunities for perpetrators to rejoin society as functioning members. In contrast, we expend resources toward "treating" victims to turn them into successful survivors and in the process of doing so instill their dependency on the state. We do this by requiring victims who seek support and protection from the state to comply with authorities, which in many cases are social workers, and acquiesce to the invasion of state control into their lives. In return for protection and assistance, needy women and children often relinquish control of their own lives and are forced to become individuals who need constant over-sight and regulation. "As women have become the subjects of a more expansive welfare state, social service agencies have viewed women and their needs in ways that have often discouraged them from resisting regulations and from being active participants in their own decisions" (Bumiller, 2008). Some social workers use professional authority to support a deficit approach that allows social workers to scrutinize the parenting skills, education, housing, relationships, and psychological coping skills of those who have experienced sexual violence and then prescribe behaviors necessary to access to benefits. Those who voice complaints and resist scrutiny may be denied benefits such as disqualifying women from TANF benefits who fail to comply with work requirements or cutting off assistance to women who return to violent relationships. As key actors in this process, social workers have the opportunity to legitimize women's voice both within social welfare institutions and within the confines of relationships rather than reinforcing dependency and in some circumstances, revictimizing the individuals by making compliance a prerequisite for assistance.

The commonality of these examples lies in the omission of a normative frame that transcends national borders. The foundation of a rights-based approach is nested in universal legal guarantees to protect individuals and groups against the actions and omissions that interfere with fundamental freedoms, entitlements, and human dignity as first presented in the Universal Declaration of Human Rights (United Nations, 1948). International human rights law is based on a series of international conventions, covenants, and treaties ratified by states as well as other nonbinding instruments such as declarations, guidelines, and principles. Taken together, these inalienable, interdependent, interrelated, and indivisible human rights are owned by people everywhere and responsibility to respect, protect, and fulfill these rights is primarily the obligation of the state.

Bonding social work practice to these international legal instruments obligates social workers to look beyond their own government's responses to social issues, to empower the populations they work with to have their voice heard, and to recast the neglected sovereignty of marginalized individuals and communities. It moves social workers away from being agents of the state to being change agents in keeping with the founding vision of social work. It reunites the different methods of social work practice by obligating all social workers to reflect on how public policies affect the rights of individuals and communities as well as how individual actions affect the rights of others (see Table 2). A rights-based approach compels social workers to look beyond existing methods of helping that too often exist to justify state intervention without addressing the root causes of the situation. It calls upon social workers who often act as agents of the state to acknowledge and act on their responsibility as moral duty bearers who have the obligation to respect, protect, and fulfill the rights of rights holders.

Rights-based approaches in social work have gained international acceptance in the past two decades, more so outside of the United States than within. Social workers in the United States are relatively new to human rights practice, in part because of longstanding resistance known as "American exceptionalism" which allows the United States to initiate and even demand compliance of human rights abroad while repeatedly rejecting the application of international standards for human rights in the United States (Hertel & Libal, 2011). Most Americans are knowledgeable about civil and political rights, yet far fewer are as familiar with economic, social, and cultural rights. Relatively limited engagement in this area by social workers also stems from the perception that human rights activism is best led and achieved by lawyers or elite policy advocates. The books in this series are written to facilitate rights-based approaches to social work practice both in the United States and around the world and recognize that exposure to human rights multilateral treaties and applications may vary depending on where the reader was educated or trained.

Table 2 Rights-based approaches to social work practice at different levels of intervention

Individuals seeking assistance are not judged to be worthy or unworthy of assistance but rather are viewed as rights holders. Social workers assist others in claiming their rights and helping others understand how individual rights have been violated. Interventions offered are not patronizing or stigmatizing, rather methods provide assistance based on the dignity of and respect for all individuals Example of individual-centered change: *Sexually trafficked persons are viewed as rights holders whose rights were violated rather than as criminals and are offered healing services and other benefits to restore their wholeness*
Community/group/organization efforts are redirected away from proving that they deserve or need a resource toward learning about how they can claim their entitlements to resources. Social workers facilitate human rights education among group members including knowledge of human rights instruments, principles, and methods for accessing rights Example of group-centered change: *Groups are offered opportunities to learn about their housing rights and the change process in their community, and learn skills so that they can claim their right to participation in community decision-making*
Society redirects its social policies and goals to facilitate the realization of human rights including addressing human needs. Macropracticing social workers affect the policy process and goals by expanding means for all members of a society to have their voices heard in the decision-making process Example of society-centered change: *Persons with disabilities are able to participate in the policy-making process through the use of technology that allows them to participate in meetings from their homes*

A rights-based approach brings a holistic perspective with regards to civil, political, social, economic, and cultural roles we hold as human beings and a more holistic understanding of well-being that goes beyond the meeting of material needs. Our understanding of human rights is always evolving, and our methods, practices, research, interventions, and processes should evolve as our understanding deepens. The purpose of this series is to assist social work practitioners, educators, and students toward operationalizing a new approach to social work practice that is grounded in human rights. It is hoped that the books will stimulate discussion and the introduction of new methods of practice around maximizing the potential of individuals, communities, and societies. The books, like social work, reflect the wide range of practice methods, social issues, and populations while specifically addressing an essential area of social work practice. By using current issues as examples of rights-based approaches, the books facilitate the ability of social workers familiar with human rights to apply rights-based approaches in their practice. Each book in the series calls on social work practitioners in clinical, community, research, or policy-making settings to be knowledgeable about the laws in their jurisdiction but to also look beyond and hold states accountable to the international human rights laws and framework.

Fordham University
New York, NY, USA

Shirley Gatenio Gabel

References

Abramovitz, M. (1998). Social work and social reform: An arena of struggle. *Social Work, 43*(6), 512–526.

Austin, M. J., & Ezell, M. (2004). Educating future social work administrators. *Administration in Social Work, 28*(1), 1–3.

Bumiller, K. (2008). *In an abusive state: How neoliberalism appropriated the feminist movement against sexual violence*. Durham: Duke University Press.

Chapin, R. (1995). Social policy development: The strengths perspective. *Social Work, 40*(4), 506–514.

Early, T., & GlenMaye, L. (2000). Valuing families: Social work practice with families from a strengths perspective. *Social Work, 45*(2), 118–130.

Friedman, M., & Friedman, B. (2006). *Settlement houses: Improving the welfare of America's immigrants*. New York: Rosen Publishing.

Hauss, G., & Schulte, D. (Eds.). (2009). *Amid social contradictions: Towards a history of social work in Europe*. Opladen, Farmington Hills, MI: Barbara Budrich Publishers.

Healy, L. M. (2008). Exploring the history of social work as a human rights profession. *International Social Work, 51*(6), 735–746.

Hertel, S., & Libal, K. (2011). *Human Rights in the United States: Beyond Exceptionalism*. Cambridge.

Iarskaia-Smirnova, E., & Romanov, P. (2009). Rhetoric and practice of modernisation: Soviet social policy (1917–1930). In G. Hauss & D. Schulte (Eds.), *Amid social contradictions: Towards a history of social work in Europe*. Farmington Hills, MI: Barbara Budrich Publishers.
Ife, J. (2012). *Human rights and social work: Towards rights-based practice*. Cambridge: Cambridge University Press.
Johnson, S., & Moorhead, B. (2011). Social eugenics practices with children in Hitler's Nazi Germany and the role of social work: Lessons for current practice. *Journal of Social Work Values and Ethics, 8*(1). http://www.jswve.org
Kisthardt, W. (1992). A strengths model of case management: The principles and functions of a helping partnership with persons with persistent mental illness. In D. Saleebey (Ed.), *The strengths perspective in social work practice*. New York: Longman.
Knee, R. T., & Folsom, J. (2012). Bridging the crevasse between direct practice social work and management by increasing the transferability of core skills. *Administration in Social Work, 36*, 390–408.
Kruse, E. (2009). Toward a history of social work training Germany—discourses and struggle for power at the turning points. In G. Hauss & D. Schulte (Eds.), *Amid social contradictions: Towards a history of social work in Europe*. Farmington Hills, MI: Barbara Budrich Publishers.
Melinz, G. (2009). In the interest of children: Modes of intervention in family privacy in Austria (1914–1945). In G. Hauss & D. Schulte (Eds.), *Amid social contradictions: Towards a history of social work in Europe*. Farmington Hills, MI: Barbara Budrich Publishers.
Morris, P. M. (2008). Reinterpreting Abraham Flexner's speech, 'Is social work a profession?' Its meaning and influence on the field's early professional development. *Social Service Review, 82* (1), 29–60.
Platt, A. M. (1965). *The child savers: The invention of delinquency*. Chicago, IL: University of Chicago Press.
Saleebey, D. (1992a). Introduction: Beginnings of a strengths approach to practice. In D. Saleebey (Ed.), *The strengths perspective in social work practice*. New York: Longman.
Saleebey, D. (Ed.). (1992b). *The strengths perspective in social work practice*. New York: Longman.
Szikra, D. (2009). Social policy and anti-semitic exclusion before and during WW II in Hungary: The case of productive social policy. In G. Hauss & D. Schulte (Eds.), *Amid social contradictions: Towards a history of social work in Europe*. Farmington Hills, MI: Barbara Budrich Publishers.
Trolander, J. A. (1987). *Professionalism and social change: from the settlement house movement to neighborhood centers, 1886 to the present*. New York: Columbia University Press.
United Nations. (1948, December 9). *Convention on the prevention and punishment of genocide*. Retrieved from http://www.ohchr.org/EN/ProfessionalInterest/Pages/CrimeOfGenocide.aspx
United Nations. (1989, November 20). *Convention on the rights of the child*. New York: United Nations. Retrieved from http://www2.ohchr.org/english/law/pdf/crc.pdf
United Nations Office of the High Commissioner for Human Rights (UN OHCHR). (2002). Draft Guidelines for a Human Rights Approach to Poverty Reduction Strategies 2002.
United Nations. (2006, December 13). *Convention on the rights of persons with disabilities*. New York: United Nations. Retrieved from http://www2.ohchr.org/english/law/pdf/ disabilitiesconvention.pdf

Preface

Consistent with all *SpringerBriefs in Rights-Based Approaches to Social Work*, practice will be reframed from deficit models used by practitioners and alternatively will offer a human rights-based perspective. This approach to practice places an emphasis on human rights and challenges practitioners to actively engage and collaborate with populations and communities in all decision-making processes. With the increasing number of short-term study abroad trips, it is essential to offer a framework that provides strategies for empowering the populations and communities in which these trips occur; otherwise, good intentions often result in harm caused to those students and practitioners hope to help.

Within this text, we examine explanations for the missteps, which have ranged from imperialism and greed to ill-conceived planning and poorly regulated Christian impulses. Social theory may offer an alternative and perhaps more transcendent explanation for the ineffectual attempts to help, for example, providing a helping framework that emphasizes reciprocal liberation built upon solidarity, rather than charity. Pitfalls inherent to many helping professions, including standardization, generalized surveillance, and social control, will be examined as well as the calculations of cost and reward considered by both parties of an exchange. As a result, how and why one helps becomes part of a critically considered social equation.

As a profession, social work has been looking for ways to incorporate human rights concepts into its curriculum to shift away from a reliance on deficit models such as charity and needs-based approaches to practice. Strategies that are derived from human rights concepts naturally align with the core values of the social work profession in that they incorporate the values of social justice, the importance of human relationships, service to others, and the dignity and worth of all citizens.

A clear strength of our book is its accessibility and relevance to both instructors and students, with thoughtful emphasis placed in each chapter to align with the needs of each group more distinctly. Chapter 1, with its emphasis on our profession's missteps and a critique of traditional approaches to short-term study abroad trips will likely appeal directly to faculty, but its value to students and future practitioners is clear. Chapter 2 presents the human rights-based framework and is a chapter that likely will have its greatest impact when read by students, with faculty utilizing this chapter as a guide. Students will appreciate the case examples that illuminate the complex concepts that are taught by faculty as well as the specific exercises and assignments shared to guide both faculty and student through the process of developing and implementing short-term study abroad trips. Faculty will likely embrace Chapter 3, as it brings long-overdue empirical support to field instruction. Students who are sometimes weary of "evidence" and "research" will find this chapter readable and valuable for its straightforward incorporation of research that aligns with social work values. Finally, Chapter 4 will likely be of value to both faculty and students, who appreciate the wisdom and necessity of the human rights–based perspective to international and domestic learning.

This text is designed with both travel-based (field education) and classroom learning (pre-trip preparation) in mind. Though developed with more depth, theory, and evidence than a "how-to manual," this book will serve as an exemplary "guide" that prepares those engaging in short-term study abroad trips with information and strategies that are derived from the key concepts of a rights-based approach to field education. In our field, instructors may be MSW or DSW/PhD level; both groups will find this book useful and appreciate the text for field learning that incorporates a rigorous framework, clear values, and evidence related of effectiveness. DSW and PhD faculty will recognize its scholarly tone, while MSW practitioners may value its incorporation of strategies that reflect the "how to" of practice. Similarly, both undergraduate and graduate students will value the challenge and utility of this text, as it elevates the standard approach to study abroad in ways that align with global citizenship and cultural competence (familiar terms for undergraduate and graduate students alike) and embed these constructs in theory that graduate students will recognize.

The final chapter of this text extends the human rights-based framework for short-term study abroad to domestic service learning and semester-long field placements. The framework will help faculty and students who travel and study domestically to partner with communities in ways that align with the values of human dignity, participation, nondiscrimination, transparency, and accountability. Though international trips place in sharp relief the importance of values like nondiscrimination, such values are no less relevant in the increasingly diverse communities we find "at home." For semester-long study abroad trips, the human rights-based framework provides a direction and compass for the sometimes-disorienting experience of collaborating with others around the globe. Finally, though designed as a text that can provide direction for those *engaging in* learning that involves service and travel, this text may also be a valued resource to supplement classroom-based learning. It renders whole cloth the experience of study abroad—mistakes we have made and continue to make, well-supported strategies for how to correct our work, and validation of the strategies provided.

Social work education may be the vanguard for the adoption of a human rights framework, but this orientation to understanding and addressing significant world problems is becoming part of the broad educational landscape. As noted above, international study is de rigueur at most universities and many majors incorporate international travel and "service trips" in their educational plans. This text is a social work text in that social work values align with the human rights-based approach to study and "service" abroad. However, its relevance transcends the social work discipline as the human rights-based perspective offers a framework for *all* international work and a "how to" guide for other educational disciplines.

Millersville, PA, USA

Karen Rice
Heather Girvin

Contents

About the Authors

Karen Rice obtained her MSW from Temple University in 2000 and her PhD in 2011 from the University of Maryland, Baltimore. She serves as the Chair of the School of Social Work at Millersville University of Pennsylvania, where she has been on faculty since 2006. She teaches research, statistics, diversity, and international social work to students across all three levels (BSW, MSW, DSW) of social work education. Utilizing a social justice and human rights framework, her research centers on ways to enhance individuals' (youth, students, adults) levels of compassion, advocacy, and dialogue across and within various social groups. Trained in Intergroup Dialogue, Dr. Rice conducts trainings and co-facilitates dialogues to raise awareness, foster understanding and appreciation, build alliances, and develop individual and collective efforts to promote positive social change. Additionally, her ongoing research and practice centers on the creation of diverse, equitable, and inclusive policies, practices, and programs within institutions and communities, domestically and internationally. Whenever possible, she employs expressive arts to examine and explore these issues as well as to raise awareness, impart knowledge, and promote positive social change. Dr. Rice is the co-founder of Global Champions 4 Humanity, a summer youth program fostering global citizenship.

Heather Girvin earned her MSS from Bryn Mawr Graduate School of Social Work and Social Research in 1995 and returned to earn her PhD in 2002. Dr. Girvin joined the faculty of the Millersville University School of Social Work in Millersville, Pennsylvania in 2007. She teaches social theory, family violence, child welfare, and diversity across all three levels of social work education (BSW, MSW, DSW). In her research, Dr. Girvin implements a human rights-based perspective that centers on social justice, while exploring trauma-related to broadly defined violence. Dr. Girvin's current research interests include alternatives to traditional social services and therapies, with particular interest in animal-assisted therapies and the expressive arts. Dr. Girvin is particularly interested in the development of strategies that span the levels of intervention, resist the premature medicalization of problems, and incorporate compassion and solidarity rather than "service implementation." She is the founder of Lone Oak Animal-Assisted Therapy and Educational Services, an equine-assisted therapeutic services and educational non-profit program.

Chapter 1
Finding Our Framework

The *SpringerBriefs in Rights-Based Approaches to Social Work* reframe deficit models used by practitioners and offer a human rights-based perspective to practice (Gatenio Gabel, 2016). This approach to practice emphasizes human rights and challenges practitioners to engage actively and collaborate with populations and communities in all decision-making processes. The call for practitioners to use a human rights-based approach to practice requires social workers to adjust current practices and necessitates a shift in social work education. Field education, the cornerstone of social work curricula, is ripe for curricular changes that reflect a human rights perspective, but shifting paradigms from "helping others, who have problems" to "working with others" may be lacking. This Brief aims to address that gap.

The Council on Social Work Education's Educational Policy and Accreditation Standards (EPAS) (CSWE, 2015) guide social work education inside the classrooms of accredited programs, as well as in the field. The CSWE identifies field education as the signature pedagogy for social work education and describes signature pedagogies as having components of instruction that familiarize future practitioners with the standards of professional practice. These standards allow social work students to demonstrate behaviors equivalent to those expected of experienced social work practitioners while still learning. CSWE directs schools to evaluate students' ability to demonstrate the knowledge, skill, and affect that corresponds to each standard, as appropriate for a particular level of education.

An increasing number of social work programs are offering short-term study abroad experiences as part of field education. In theory, these experiences will provide students with opportunities to embrace learning articulated by the Council on Social Work Education's EPAS (CSWE, 2015). The EPAS require social work programs to demonstrate that their graduates are able to "engage diversity and difference in practice," including being able to "understand the forms and mechanisms of oppression and discrimination and recognize the extent to which a culture's structures and values, including social, economic, political, and cultural exclusions, may

K. Rice, H. Girvin, *Human Rights-Based Approach to Short-Term Study Abroad*, SpringerBriefs in Rights-Based Approaches to Social Work,
https://doi.org/10.1007/978-3-030-87421-6_1

oppress, marginalize, alienate, or create privilege and power." Despite the elevated position of field education in CSWE's view of social work curricula, the organization does not offer a specific theoretical or practice framework to guide its development and implementation. As a result, students might unintentionally approach field education utilizing deficit models of practice or adopt a strength-based perspective, which is familiar in social work education and practice. Both approaches have limitations. The deficit model—a paradigm that focuses on clients' problems and limitations—has a legacy in social work practice. Though since replaced in most textbooks and curricula by other models and conceptualizations, its influence persists. Lapierre (2008), for example, discusses the powerful deficit-based discourse that surrounds mothers and mothering in the context of poverty. McGovern (2011) argues that knowledge gaps and practice limitations in gerontology and work with patients with dementia result from a deficit paradigm. Finally, Fullagar and O'Brien (2014) call for a paradigmatic shift away from deficit models of depression to a social recovery model that emphasizes women's capacity and connections to their communities.

Contemporary social work curricula are typically designed to mitigate the stigma of "deficit thinking," and many social work practice classes include the strengths-based perspective as an essential model for social work practice (Probst, 2010). Adopting a strengths-based perspective in social work practice has been heralded as the "solution" to the negativity of deficit models of practice. Saleebey's (1996) groundbreaking work on a strengths-based approach to social work practice highlighted the profession's tendency to identify problems and diagnose, often to the exclusion of assessment that identified clients' strengths. In Saleebey's view, the inclination to see issues to the exclusion of growth capacity shaped social work for many years across practice fields and modalities. Saleebey describes the helping professions as "saturated with psychosocial approaches based on individual, family, and community pathology, deficits, problems, abnormality, victimization, and disorder" (p. 296). In particular, the strengths-based perspective is viewed as effective in diversity education. Spiteri (2016) explores the importance of strengths-based narratives across multicultural settings, highlighting their importance to effective intercultural communication. The dovetailing of a strengths-based perspective and social work curricula content related to diversity might have particular relevance in field education.

Despite the points of alignment between the strengths-based perspective and social work values, some have argued that this perspective may obscure reality and belie the intransigence of serious problems. In the end, a "grudge match" is created wherein social workers are asked to choose one side of a false and constructed dichotomy: Will you, practitioner, focus on problems or focus on strengths (McMillen et al., 2004)? McMillen et al. (2004) argue that the best version of social work practice maintains a dual focus on problem-solving and capacity building. However, the history of our helping efforts is marred by the misinterpretation of both foci.

A rights-based approach to practice is aligned with social work values and reflective of EPAS content. Furthermore, it is an approach that encourages true partnerships that incorporate the voices of all parties engaged in the change process.

McPherson (2020) notes that a rights-based approach to social work practice is useful (it guides intervention and assessment) and essential, as it reflects human rights principles of human dignity, nondiscrimination, participation, transparency, and accountability (Androff, 2016; McPherson & Abell, 2020). These transcendent principles resonate with EPAS standards and provide a platform for social workers to cultivate relationships built on equality and respect (McPherson, 2015).

Learning from Our Mistakes: Helping Whom, How, and Why?

Short-term study abroad trips, an increasingly popular component of field education, can—as noted above—support students in their efforts to achieve CSWE competencies, particularly related to "engaging diversity and difference in practice" (Mapp, 2012). In addition, the trips have the potential to teach participants about the structural causes of and different societal responses to global social issues such as poverty, child maltreatment, and human trafficking. However, if not done correctly, short-term study abroad trips can perpetuate stereotypes and the idea of the American as a "savior" and reinforce needs-based or deficit models of practice. In a needs-based or deficit view of short-term study abroad trips, members of the host community may be conceptualized as individuals with deficits who need help. Indeed, many international charitable organizations do that despite good intentions.

Many of the transnational organizations that provide assistance utilize the deficit model. Across helping professions, the motivation for helping has ranged from corruption to ill-conceived notions of service to poorly regulated Christian impulses (Corbett & Fikkert, 2009). Attempts to "save Haiti" are painfully illustrative of all of these motives. Corbett and Fikkert's (2009) critical examination of Christian churches' philanthropic service trips adopts a Biblical perspective and argues that though the church's mission includes helping the poor, the definition of poverty will change depending on who is defining it. While communities "receiving help" may highlight the social scope of their poverty, wealthy North American churches emphasize the lack of material things or geographical location. The authors posit that this causes a harmful cycle wherein North American churches provide material resources and evangelism to "the poor." In doing so, they reinforce the "poor people's" sense of inferiority and lowered self-esteem.

Many other well-intentioned institutions may be helping in ways that are effective or do not respect human rights. According to the National Center for Charitable Statistics (NCCS), there are more than 1.5 million nonprofit organizations in the United States, including public charities, private foundations, and other types of nonprofit organizations, including chambers of commerce, fraternal organizations, and civic leagues (NCCS, 2019). Many of these organizations are involved in efforts to "help poor communities" outside the United States and have failed to produce evidence that their work has fundamentally changed the life quality of communities they aim to assist. In the worst cases, corruption has derailed helping. For example, the American Red Cross raised nearly $500 million after the 2010 earthquake in Haiti, more than any other nonprofit. A significant portion of this money was supposedly earmarked for an ambitious plan to build housing, but in the end, only six permanent homes were constructed (https://www.npr.org/2016/06/16/482020436/senators-report-finds-fundamental-concerns-about-red-cross-finances). Perhaps making matters worse, a quarter of the money people donated immediately following the earthquake—nearly $125 million—was spent on the American Red Cross's internal expenses. The charity built upon false promises and exploitation aligns with the deficit models to helping rather than a rights-based approach to help, which is built upon solidarity.

Short-term trips abroad involving social work students and faculty have likely not resulted in such flagrantly ill-conceived "helping plans." However, students may knowingly or unknowingly adopt strength- or deficit-based models, neither of which provide necessary guidance. Likewise, students adopting a combined perspective, seeing some strengths and some areas of development, are left with a dual focus that provides no overarching rationale. Of equal importance, neither model reflects contemporary CSWE standards, and both ignore calls for collaborative models of helping.

The primacy of student learning may be wrongheaded and lead to the genuine possibility that harm—camouflaged as helping, education, and good intentions—becomes the result of trips abroad. For students, harm may be difficult to identify, as good intention can obscure outcomes. Offered resources may require changes in behavior or cultural practices. Programs may reflect values that do not align with the host culture. Students may work hard and learn, but these objectives can neglect the host community's preferences that are providing the learning. "Voluntourism" is a term used in the literature to characterize those short-term study abroad trips that cause more harm to a community than aid (e.g., Bargeman, Richards, & Govers, 2016). The damage caused by voluntourism is partly due to assigning students the role of experts (because they are from the United States) and allowing the use of "helping" practices that magnify cultural differences rather than building upon areas of commonality.

What We Already Know: The Lessons of Social Theory

Given some common assumptions about human nature, perhaps it is not shocking that greed, unregulated philanthropic impulses, unethical behavior, or poor planning have thwarted some well-publicized organizational attempts to "help others." Though far less likely to occur during faculty-led, short-term study abroad trips, the same misleading impulses, as well as both deficit- and strengths-based thinking could lead to preventable missteps. Moreover, existing theoretical frameworks illuminate the dynamics and conditions that may lead to such errors. Social theory (e.g., Blau, 1964; Foucault, 1980; Freire, 1970) may offer an alternative and perhaps more transcendent explanation for the ineffectual attempts to help. Liberation theologist and theorist Paulo Freire (1970), for example, provides a helping framework that emphasizes reciprocal liberation built upon solidarity rather than charity or "false generosity." According to Freire, stop-gap "help" that meets immediate needs dehumanizes the "helpers," allowing them to maintain their elevated position, thereby distancing them from their human connection to those they aim to help. Their assuaged conscience undercuts their motivation to partner in the facilitation of change. In turn, the helped are "taught" that their positions as persons "in need of help" are idiosyncratic or individualized, rather than the result of systemic oppression. Humans seeking assistance are stigmatized and denied basic human dignity. In the end, the dynamics that support or justify social and economic injustice are covered and bolstered by misguided attempts at helping.

Michel Foucault (1980) reminds us of the pitfalls inherent to many helping professions, including standardization, generalized surveillance, and social control. Foucault cautions that inherent in all helping professions is a hierarchy that places the helper in an elevated position protected by discourse and professional boundaries. From that higher status, the helpers offer assistance but require "appropriate behaviors" that align with socially constructed standards of health, civility, and citizenship. Those standards are co-created by the helpers, who do not seek to collaborate with the individuals receiving help but rather compliance and acquiescence.

Blau (1964) reminds us that both parties in an exchange are involved in calculations of cost and reward; thus, how and why one helps becomes part of a critically considered social equation. Blau believed that all social interactions are shaped by a reciprocal exchange of both tangible and intangible rewards. Such social activities entail some cost to the actor, but each tries to minimize the cost and has expectations about what should be received in return. When applied to helping professions, motivations for helping run the gamut from professional ethics to self-aggrandizement. What seems clear in Blau's work is that even noble philanthropies or trained professionals may engage in an assessment process that connects helping relationships and ideas of service to less laudable objectives, such as professional achievement, successful outcomes, or perhaps receipt of personal gratitude. Absent strategies to ensure transparency or accountability, it seems likely that "helpers" may be vulnerable to what Blau would consider natural tendencies to improve their standing instead of or along with those of whom they aim to help.

The theories summarized above highlight pitfalls inherent to helping strategies. On their own merit, each theory highlights tendencies that helping professionals may seek to avoid. While such theoretical implications may offer practice wisdom, it is not straightforward to draw from their inverse to construct a proactive framework that could guide social work practice and social work field education. However, the human rights-based perspective incorporates the lessons learned while providing a proactive framework that centers on dimensions of social justice (e.g., economic justice and environmental justice).

The Human Rights-Based Perspective

Neither deficit–/needs-based nor strengths-based approaches have adequately guided social work education, including short-term study abroad trips. They create a human rights framework that may fill the gap created by CSWE objectives that align with our profession's code of ethics but fail to include a guiding framework for field education experiences, such as short-term trips abroad. A human rights-based framework aligns with the core values of the social work profession. Such a methodology incorporates the values of social justice, the importance of human relationships, service to others, and the dignity and worth of all citizens (National Association of Social Workers, 2008). Further, this framework provides protective factors that decrease the likelihood that social workers traveling abroad will be derailed by antiquated perspectives (e.g., strengths-based or deficit-based models) that do not reflect fully the complexity and reciprocity associated with meaningful, ethical, social change.

As a profession rooted in advocacy, social justice, and human rights, it is essential that short-term study abroad trips be guided by efforts to help empower community members rather than provide charity that fosters dependence and reinforces status differentials. To do so requires utilization of a framework that replaces our habits of "charity" and "helping" with a commitment to joining in solidarity to promote change in service of social justice. This framework should include individuals within the communities where the service learning occurs as failure to include those being affected by the service-learning activities as full partners can reduce efforts and perpetuate social injustices (Fisher & Grettenberger, 2015). The key concepts of the human rights-based approach to practice that will guide our framework are human dignity, participation, nondiscrimination, transparency, and accountability (Androff, 2016). To avoid exploiting members of the host country and perpetuating harmful social work practices, it is essential to hold ourselves accountable in the design and implementation of short-term study abroad trips. In doing so, the aim of short-term study abroad trips is on social justice and human rights, and this textbook offers the human rights-based framework as an approach when developing and implementing short-term study abroad trips.

Increased Number, Increased Need

Today's social movements (e.g., Black Lives Matter) are calling for an accurate retelling of that heritage, one that acknowledges true structures and motivations. Too much of the US "international history" can be described as the intentional (though obfuscated) extension of power. Daniel Immerwahr (2019) has discussed the "forthright spirit of imperialism" that led to the US "acquisition" of Puerto Rico,

Hawaii, the Philippines, Guam, American Samoa, and Wake and at the turn of the twentieth century eventually came under scrutiny and references to "colonies" was replaced with discussions of "territories." The move from territories to colonies to neocolonialism (through which dominant countries use economic, political, and cultural pressures to influence other countries) has happened quite rapidly, and versions of that process tend to minimize the amount of territory the United States actually controls (Immerwahr, 2019). US theoretical linguist and social critic Noam Chomsky has repeatedly described the United States as an empire, joining others in pointing to the dispossession of Native Americans and relegation of many of them to reservations, the military seizure of Mexico, the utter and violent subordination of African Americans, and the spread of US economic power abroad as clear indicators of imperialism. Certainly, we are not suggesting that all international involvements are built around intentions of dominance and control, but they *do* have to reckon with that legacy.

The skepticism with which citizens of the United States are received abroad has been well-earned, and recent instances of racially motivated violence have amplified global concerns related to justice and well-being in the United States. This is not an inconsequential point. The sheer number of Americans traveling abroad—with claims that they want to "help," but carrying the baggage of our history—demands our attention. In his study of overseas volunteering in the United States between 2004 and 2012, Lough (2013) found that an average of 900,000 Americans volunteer abroad every year. Beyond the field requirements of social work education, universities, in general, attract students with their "travel packages." Even college admissions are affected by volunteer travel and service during "gap years." According to Waxman (n.d.), international service trips have become a common strategy used by college applicants to demonstrate their values, passion, uniqueness, and a dedication to service that will hopefully obscure applicants' privilege to admissions counselors. Even corporations are "incentivizing" international service. Many companies have corporate social responsibility policies. A 2013 report issued by the Committee to Encourage Corporate Philanthropy committee surveyed 240 companies (including 60 of the largest 100 companies on the Fortune 500 list) and found that just under half have a formal international volunteer program.

With so many individuals from the United States traveling abroad, we who are in a profession that pursues justice and human rights globally have an important role to play. As social workers, social work trainers, social work trip leaders, and social work educators, we have a vital contribution to make. Given our familiarity with the exploitive nature of historical "charity" endeavors, as well as our professional mandate to seek human justice, we have an opportunity and obligation to prepare students who go abroad to "serve" from a human rights-based perspective that celebrates and protects human dignity, seeks participation and collaboration, adheres to the highest standards of accountability and transparency, and employs strategies that are inclusive and collaborative.

Summary

Short-term study abroad is an increasingly popular component of social work education programs. Too often, the focus of such trips is developed out of a needs-based or deficit view where members of the host community may be conceptualized as individuals with deficits who need help. Indeed, many international charitable organizations do that despite good intentions. CSWE directs schools to provide students with opportunities to engage diversity and difference in practice. Field education, the cornerstone of social work curricula, is ripe for curricular changes that reflect a human rights perspective, but shifting paradigms from "helping others, who have problems" to "working with others" may be lacking. The call for practitioners to use a human rights-based approach to practice requires social workers to adjust current practices and necessitates a shift in social work education. A human rights-based approach to practice is aligned with social work values and reflective of EPAS content. Furthermore, it is an approach that encourages true partnerships that incorporate the voices of all parties engaged in the change process.

Exercises

1. Consider your social work practice or your conceptualization of service. Can you recall a time when you operated from a strengths-based or deficit-based perspective? How might the implementation of the human rights-based framework help to guide your practice?
2. Before moving forward in this text, imagine the ways that a human rights-based framework might help you to work more ethically in practice, teaching, and volunteer service. Do the pillars of the human rights-based approach—human dignity, nondiscrimination, participation, transparency, and accountability—lead you to think differently about the professional or volunteer work that you do?
3. Identify an international study abroad program and visit its website. Assess the extent to which it promotes a deficit-based, needs-based, strengths-based, and/or rights-based approach to helping.

References

Admin. (2018, November). The changing trends of volunteer travel. http://learningservice.info/the-changing-trends-of-volunteer-travel/

Androff, D. (2016). *Practicing rights: Human rights-based approaches to social work practice*. Routledge.

Bargeman, B., Richards, G., & Govers, E. (2018). Volunteer tourism impacts in Ghana: A practice approach. *Current Issues in Tourism, 21*, 1486-1501, https://doi.org/10.1080/13683500.2015.1137277.

Blau, P. M. (1964). Social exchange theory. Retrieved September, 3(2007), 62.
Committee on Encouraging Corporate Philanthropy. (2013). http://cecp.co/research/benchmarking-reports/giving-in-numbers.html
Corbett, S., & Fikkert, B. (2009). *When helping hurts: How to alleviate poverty without hurting the poor–and yourself.* Moody Publishers.
CSWE. (2015). https://www.cswe.org/Accreditation/Standards-and-policies/2015-EPAS
Fisher, C., & Grettenberger, S. (2015, July). Community-based participatory study abroad: A proposed model for social work education. *Journal of Social Work Education, 51*(3), 566–582.
Foucault, M. (1980). Power/Knowledge: Selected Interviews and Other Writings. New York City: Pantheon Books.
Freire, P. (1970). Pedagogy of the oppressed. New York: Continuum.
Fullagar, S., & O'Brien, W. (2014) Social recovery and the move beyond deficit models of depression: A feminist analysis of mid-life women's self-care practices. Social Science & Medicine, 117, p. 116-124.
Gabel S.G. (2016). Understanding Human Rights and Social Policy. In: A Rights-Based Approach to Social Policy Analysis. SpringerBriefs in Rights-Based Approaches to Social Work. Springer, Cham. https://doi.org/10.1007/978-3-319-24412-9_2.
Immerwahr, D.. (2019, February). The United States likes to think of itself as a republic, but it holds territories all over the world. https://www.theguardian.com/news/2019/feb/15/the-us-hidden-empire-overseas-territories-united-states-guam-puerto-rico-american-samoa
Lapierre, S. (2008). Mothering in the context of domestic violence: The pervasiveness of a deficit model of mothering. Child & Family Social Work, 13, p. 454-463.
Lough, B. J. (2013). International Volunteering from the United States between 2004 and 2012. CSD Research Brief, (13–14). Retrieved from http://csd.wustl.edu/Publications/Documents/RB13-14.pdf
Mapp, S. (2012). Effect of short-term study abroad programs on students' cultural adaptability. *Journal of Social Work Education, 48*(4), 727–737.
McGovern, J. (2011, October). Couple meaning-making and dementia: Challenges to the deficit model. *Journal of Gerontological Social Work, 54*(7), 678–690.
McMillen, J. C., Morris, L., & Sherraden, M. (2004). Ending social work's grudge match: Problems versus strengths. *Families in Society: The Journal of Contemporary Social Service, 8*(3), 317–325.
McPherson, J. (2015). Human rights practice in social work: A U.S. social worker looks to Brazil for leadership. *European Journal of Social Work, 18*(4), 599–612. https://doi.org/10.1080/13691457.2014.947245
McPherson, J. (2020, June). Now is the time for a rights-based approach to social work practice. *Journal of Human Rights Social Work, 5*(3), 1–3. https://doi.org/10.1007/s41134-020-00125-1
McPherson, J., & Abell, N. (2020). Measuring rights-based practice: Introducing the human rights methods in social work scales. *British Journal of Social Work, 50*(1), 222–242. https://doi.org/10.1093/bjsw/bcz132. https://www.socialworkers.org/
National Association of Social Workers. (2008). Code of Ethics. Author.
NCCS. (2019). https://nccs.urban.org/
Probst, B. (2010). Implicit and explicit use of the strengths perspective in social work education. *Journal of Teaching in Social Work, 30*, 468-484, https://doi.org/10.1080/08841233.2010.515921
Saleebey, D. (1996). The strengths perspective in social work practice: Extensions and cautions. *Social Work, 41*, 296–305.
Spiteri, D. (2016). Multiculturalism, higher education, and intercultural communication: Developing strengths-based narratives for teaching and learning. Springer..
Waxman, B. (n.d.). The Faux Pas of the Well-Intentioned Westerner, A peek into the realities of "helping those less privileged. https://medium.com/@beccawax/the-faux-pas-of-the-well-intentioned-westerner-fc0de6f45c1e

Chapter 2
Applying a Human Rights-Based Framework

As highlighted in Chap. 1, despite good intentions, rigorous training, and professional competence, attempts to help vulnerable groups and individuals are too often unsuccessful at best, damaging at worst. Explanations for the missteps have ranged from imperialism and greed to ill-conceived planning and poorly regulated Christian impulses (Corbett & Fikkert, 2012). Social theorists (e.g., Blau, 1964; Foucault, 1980; Freire, 1970) offer alternative and perhaps more transcendent insights for the reasons that short-term learning trips may fail. Paulo Freire (1970), for example, explains to us effort built on "false generosity" or charity rather than solidarity and liberation will prolong and deepen inequities. According to Foucault (1980), relying on standardization also thwart efforts to transform because it can often result in social control. Social exchange theorists (Blau, 1964) remind us that both parties of an exchange are involved in calculations of cost and reward; as a result, how and why one helps becomes part of a critically considered social equation. These theorists highlight the importance of our actions on others and why rights-based approaches should be applied to developing and implementing short-term study abroad trips.

As a profession rooted in advocacy, social justice, and human rights, short-term study abroad trips must be guided by efforts to help empower community members rather than provide charity that fosters dependence, reinforces status differentials, and makes authentic collaboration unlikely. To do so requires the utilization of a framework that replaces our habits of "charity" and "helping" with a commitment to joining in solidarity to promote change in the service of social justice. This framework should include individuals within the communities where the service learning occurs as failure to include those affected by the service learning activities as full partners can reduce efforts and perpetuate social injustices (Fisher & Grettenberger, 2015).

It is essential to hold ourselves accountable in the design and implementation of short-term study abroad trips to avoid exploiting members of the host country and

K. Rice, H. Girvin, *Human Rights-Based Approach to Short-Term Study Abroad*,
SpringerBriefs in Rights-Based Approaches to Social Work,
https://doi.org/10.1007/978-3-030-87421-6_2

perpetuating harmful social practices. Brown (2001) and Mitchell (2015) report that short-term study abroad trips need to create university and community partnerships that place the community's needs in which the service learning will occur as equal to that of the needs of the students' learning. This approach, critical service learning, redistributes power and develops authentic relationships (Mitchell, 2015). In doing so, the aim of short-term study abroad trips is on social justice and human rights.

Human rights-based approaches are not only consistent with the core values of social work in that such a methodology incorporates the values of social justice, the importance of human relationships, service to others, and the dignity and worth of all citizens (National Association of Social Workers, 2017), but a human rights-based approach to social work practice aligns with the critical service learning model. The key components of human rights-based approach to service learning are human dignity, nondiscrimination, participation, transparency, and accountability (Androff, 2016).

This chapter will define these key components and then apply this framework to the pre-departure, in-country, and reentry aspects of short-term study abroad planning and implementation. In doing so, the suggested activities and approaches employ a human rights-based approach to foster a collaborative, reciprocal, and respectful relationship between the university and host country members and avoid exploitation, voluntourism, and charity-based practices that emerge and outlined in the previous chapter. These attributes (collaboration, respect for others, reciprocal relationships) foster global citizenship, recognizing the interconnectedness of human lives beyond national borders (see Fig. 2.1).

When applying a human rights-based approach to short-term study abroad trips, both intrinsic and extrinsic values are experienced. Intrinsically, a human rights-based approach engages individuals from the host country as "rights-holders with entitlements" (United Nations High Commissioner for Human Rights, 2006, p. 24). As a result, "helping" becomes collaborative rather than charitable or needs-based, and the individuals from the host country not only have a specific right to assistance as a member of society but have the right to voice and guide the development of that short-term study abroad trip. When key concepts of the human rights-based approach are applied to the design and implementation of short-term study abroad trips, extrinsically the community is strengthened because individuals, when collaboratively engaged, build capacity to meet future needs and contribute positively to the enhancement of society (United Nations High Commissioner for Human Rights, 2006). What follows is an overview of each key concept and what should be considered in the design and implementation of short-term study abroad trips. For specific

Fig. 2.1 Human rights-based framework to short-term study abroad

case examples in the design and implementation of short-term study abroad trips, refer to Mapp and Rice (2018).

Key Concepts of the Human Rights-Based Approach to Practice

As previously stated, individuals are rights-holders, and therefore any practice with individuals should be from a human rights rather than human needs approach, thus fostering the dignity and worth of the individual, a key component of the human rights-based approach (Androff, 2016). Promoting *human dignity* requires individuals to be perceived as entitled to any service provided rather than viewed as recipients of a service for charity. The avoidance of perceiving the service as charity fosters and honors the individual's self-determination (Gatenio Gabel, 2015). Self-determination, which is an individual's freedom of choice (National Association of Social Workers, 2017), shifts power from the sending country to the receiving country as the host country is no longer dependent upon the sending country to define their needs and identify the solutions (Androff, 2016). Mapp and Rice (2018) provide examples of how to engage individuals from the host country in designing and implementing the service provided to respect human dignity and avoid perceiving individuals in need of our "help," "saving," and "rescuing," all synonymous of charity or needs-based approach to practice. Acknowledging every individual's human dignity and humbly and continuously promoting their worth results in the development of global citizenship (Hartman & Kiely, 2014). Acknowledging the fundamental dignity and worth of every human being requires individuals to critically reflect and examine structures that create barriers to the realization of human rights. Therefore, the following key concepts within the human rights-based approach to practice offer a pathway to becoming a global citizen.

Human rights are fundamental, universal rights applied to every person regardless of social group identities (United Nations, 1948). Therefore, short-term study abroad trips should be inclusive and nondiscriminatory. *Nondiscrimination* avoids the perpetuation of disparities and power imbalances (Androff, 2016) that are often experienced by individuals who are the recipients of services being implemented within host countries. Nondiscriminatory practices recognize the approach to social challenges within the United States may not work in other countries, and the interventions, treatments, and approaches implemented must meet the social and cultural norms of the individuals and communities (Wronka, 2008). Therefore, practicing through a cultural humility lens is essential as it fosters respect for diversity and difference (McPherson, 2015). To apply this concept, the itinerary of short-term study abroad trips needs to include opportunities to engage with individuals in the host country to challenge assumptions and stereotypes to foster empathy and compassion, key to nondiscriminatory practice. Viewing individuals in the host country as informants and experts who can identify their own needs and solutions simultaneously dissolves hierarchies and respects the dignity and worth of the individuals, consistent with Freire's (1970) social theory.

Participation, the key human rights-based approach to practice concept that ensures the redistribution of power, is the process of ensuring all individuals with whom we work are engaged in the decision-making process (Androff, 2016). Taken from the disability rights movement, participation exemplifies the well-known slogan, "nothing about us, without us." This participation however must be meaningful; otherwise, it becomes an act of tokenism. Further, the participation must be reciprocal in that there is an emphasis on capacity building in order to contribute to the growth of the country rather than perpetuating the negative effects of short-term study abroad trips (Rotabi et al., 2017). Therefore, on the one hand, the individuals within the host country take the lead in guiding the service being implemented while identifying the specific knowledge and skills community members may need to ensure full engagement by all and sustainability upon trip completion. This meaningful participation gives the rights-holders access, opportunity, and ability to exercise power within their community (Androff, 2016) and assist in capacity building to prevent the exploitation of its members and the harm often caused by short-term study abroad trips (Corbett & Fikkert, 2012).

The fourth key concept of the human rights-based approach to practice is *transparency*. Transparency involves clearly articulating necessary information to make informed decisions (Androff, 2016). This access to information would include budgets, policies, itineraries, and expectations. Articulating in advance of the short-term study abroad trip these expectations avoids potential challenges; however, it is important to emphasize the need for flexibility, patience, open mindedness, and kindness throughout the trip. It is further important to identify and discuss expected behaviors and attitudes throughout the trip as this reinforces the human rights-based approach to practice and reminds participants that the goal is to learn from and collaborate with individuals in the host country rather than impose, exploit, and disrespect.

Aligning with transparency is the final key concept of the human rights-based approach to practice, *accountability*. Accountability ensures the service provided and all interactions with individuals in the country be carried out to promote social justice and human rights (Androff, 2016). For this to occur, short-term study abroad trip leaders should prepare students in advance of the trip and outline expectations regarding behavior and attitude. This not only reinforces expected individual behavior and attitudes but fosters group accountability as it provides an opportunity for trip leaders to remind students that they are representing themselves, their university, and their country.

Further, short-term study abroad trips need to promote global citizenship and foster responsible behavior when abroad to prevent perpetuating human rights violations that are present within the host country. Centering learning and new ways of thinking as the primary goals over providing a service reminds participants of their role as a student who is capable of acquiring new ways of doing that can be brought back to their communities to further advance human rights, domestically. The table below (Table 2.1) illustrates the alignment between the human rights-based concepts and social work practice values.

Any study abroad trip involves the partnership between three key stakeholders, the university, the host country/organization, and the students. Mapp and Rice (2018) outline how a university and host country can collaborate to design and implement human rights-based short-term study abroad trips. Short-term study abroad programs must incorporate various practices pre, during, and post-trip that promote cultural engagement and not cultural tourism (Dantas, 2007). What follows are the essential pre-departure, in-country, and reentry practices to foster cultural engagement, utilizing the key components of the human rights-based framework.

Applying the Human Rights-Based Approach to Pre-Departure Activities

Before departing on a short-term study abroad trip, there are several activities to engage, foster, and reinforce key components of the human rights-based approach to practice (see Table 2.2). The activities outlined below challenge assumptions, raise critical consciousness through critical thinking, and increase awareness and knowledge. When combined, these activities foster the development of cultural humility and global citizenship. Cultural humility is a dynamic and lifelong process that focuses on self-reflection and personal critique of assumptions and biases resulting in a respectful attitude toward individuals of other cultures (Ross, 2010).

Table 2.1 Human rights-based concepts aligned with social work practice values

Human rights-based concepts	Social work practice values
Human dignity	Dignity and worth Helping relationships Self-determination
Nondiscrimination	Inclusion Redistribution of power Cultural humility Respect Compassion Empathy
Participation	Redistribution of power Reciprocal relationship Capacity building Sustainable outcomes
Transparency	Shared governance Collaborative decision-making
Accountability	Respect Promotion of justice and human rights Open-mindedness Sustainable outcomes

Table 2.2 Pre-departure activities within a human rights-based framework

Educational goal	Activity	Human rights-based key concept
Challenge assumptions Raise critical consciousness through critical thinking Develop cultural humility Foster global citizenship	Critical reflection journals	Human dignity Nondiscrimination
Challenge assumptions Increase awareness Raise critical consciousness through critical thinking Develop cultural humility Foster global citizenship	Readings Documentaries	Human dignity Nondiscrimination
Challenge assumptions Raise critical consciousness through critical thinking Increase awareness Develop cultural humility Foster global citizenship	Pre-departure orientation and education	Human dignity Nondiscrimination Participation Transparency Accountability

Critical Reflection Journal To foster cultural humility, individuals need to engage in deliberate reflection of their values and biases. Having students begin a personal reflection journal during the pre-departure stage allows students the space to explore their perceptions in a manner that is less threatening yet reflective. They will question prior assumptions and replace many of their assumptions with new knowledge throughout the trip and upon their return. Raising critical consciousness, which occurs when challenging prior biases and replacing biases with new information, is a crucial construct of Friere's social theory and will most likely lead to a more empathic approach to practice.

Schuessler et al. (2012) reviewed 200 journal entries from 50 students who participated in a four-semester community clinical experience. Students maintained a journal of their experience, critically reflecting upon their practice with others. A major theme that emerged was cultural humility. The researchers concluded that students could not learn cultural humility in the classroom with traditional teaching methods. They required self-evaluation and awareness of one's own culture, not being the only or best one, which is a process that occurs over time through reflective practices. Specific journaling prompts are provided as part of the exercises at the end of this chapter. To maximize outcomes from this exercise, students should first reflect upon the prompts before engaging in other pre-departure activities. It is essential to provide students with an opportunity to document their thoughts and feelings prior to introducing new knowledge and information.

Readings and Documentaries Participants should reflect upon their thoughts and feelings about the travel destination, the individuals, and the community where the volunteering will occur and the definition of service and the meaning of it. Following this, it is essential to introduce new knowledge and information. This knowledge should offer political, social, and historical context related to the area in which the trip will occur and the individuals who reside there. Further, students should be exposed to the relevant human rights challenges associated with the host country, signed treaties and conventions, as well as the country's response to the human rights' violations. This context raises awareness and critical consciousness in addition to challenging assumptions and existing biases.

Dutko's (2016) dissertation examined how graduate students in higher education within one program moved along the critical consciousness pathway. Critical consciousness requires one to be able to think critically, specifically to see and judge (Dutko, 2016), for the purpose to then act on issues of injustice to create social change. Dutko shared various student engagement models to foster critical consciousness, including the use of media such as film, music, and documentaries. The use of media has specific appeal in a human rights-based framework due to its potential to build critical thinking skills as it aids in the understanding of difficult and complex concepts. Coupling documentary viewing with written material such as textbooks, memoirs, and journal articles illuminates these real-world events, which is essential in the development of critical consciousness (Berk, 2009; Marcus & Stoddard, 2009).

Watts et al. (2002) exposed students to hip-hop videos along with a series of questions to reflect upon afterward. As students engaged in collective dialogue utilizing critical thinking skills, their understanding of the topic increased, and students challenged their prior assumptions about masculinity, thus raising critical consciousness. Hooks and Sealey (2001) describe films as one of the best tools of critical pedagogy as they deconstruct the complexities of the issues in a way that is viewed differently than previously considered.

Pre-Departure Orientation and Education Pre-departure orientations may vary from a few hours session discussing international travel and trip itinerary to full-semester courses exploring the concept of culture and cultural immersion. Regardless of the length of the orientation, the goal should be to help minimize fears associated with the uncertainties of traveling to an unfamiliar location to effectively meet the trip's stated outcomes. Without educating participants about the host country's culture and preparing them for how to navigate cultural differences, individuals may experience confusion and/or frustration that leads to culture shock (Gundykunst, 2003). Adler (1977) defines culture shock as

> a set of emotional reactions to the loss of perceptual reinforcements from one's own culture, to new cultural stimuli which have little or no meaning and to the misunderstanding of new and diverse experiences. It may encompass feelings of helplessness, irritability, and fears of being cheated, contaminated, injured, or disregarded. (p. 13).

NAFSA (2015), the Association of International Educators, the largest nonprofit association dedicated to international education and exchange, states that pre-departure orientations should offer practical information, culture-specific details, and academic objectives. According to Summerfield et al. (1997), teaching students how to learn is more important than providing them with the information needed to know before departing. Specifically, students need to learn how to navigate cultural confrontations by empowering them through discussions related to identity formation, cross-cultural communication, and multicultural education (Bennet, 2002; Gundykunst, 2003). Bennet (2002) suggests considering three ideas when preparing participants to study abroad. These are culture surprise, which are small but noticeable differences such as how toilets operate; culture stress is how one responds to the small events while in-country; culture shock is the realization that ideas and values within the host country are different from own. As a result, a core component of pre-departure orientation is to prepare the participants to notice and then respond to these differences to reduce stress and foster respect for and dignity toward others.

During a pre-departure meeting prior to our Costa Rica trip, it was important for us to share with our participants the expectations related to toilet use to avoid culture surprise. Despite preparing students for these expectations, some students still experienced stress related to toileting. One student, thinking the toilets were non-hygienic, was unable to utilize the bathroom. The student was definitely experiencing culture shock. Luckily, others on the trip were able to offer support and reassurance to the student that the stress experiencing was understandable, yet both practices (those performed in the home country and those performed in the host country) are hygienic when considering the practices through a cultural lens. The student was then able to consider her reactions and behaviors through the lens of another culture and was able to recognize and appreciate the differences, which reduced the stress and enhanced the student's respect toward the cultural practices of the host country. The peers demonstrated how to support each other through the transformative journey while simultaneously holding one another accountable to group expectations, a key component of the human rights-based framework.

Preparation for these differences can occur within the classroom and within one's community prior to traveling. There should be a combination of individual and group activities coupled with critical reflection (see above) and large group dialogue to explore topics such as power, privilege, positionality, race, gender, and socioeconomic status framed within the context of the United States and the country visiting. These dialogues should both challenge perspectives and assumptions and support fears and learning. Utilizing the University of Michigan's Intergroup Dialogue (https://igr.umich.edu/) framework may be one method to support this balanced approach to critically examining culture.

Pre-departure orientation offers an opportunity to foster team building among participants prior to traveling, together. Engaging in various team building activities reinforces the need of relying upon each other and working together to accomplish the trip's goals. Further, participants develop a sense of responsibility to the group and everyone's achievement, which can be articulated in a contract that participants draft outlining expectations regarding behavior. This contract, which should be added to throughout the trip and made transparent for all to see, is an example of personal and collective accountability and transparency, key concepts of the human rights-based approach to practice.

Prior to every short-term study abroad trip we lead, we host a pre-departure meeting where participants spend time getting to know one another, including names, areas of study, prior travel experience, and goals for this particular trip. During this initial pre-departure meeting, the group identifies common trip goals and then begins to frame group expectations on ensuring the goals are met. We guide the development of these group expectations by asking the participants to consider knowledge, affect, and behavior necessary to be successful. Prior to ending this initial meeting, we identify a social media platform we want to utilize to maintain contact with one another before departure. This platform serves as a "group journal" to share reflections on readings, films, and documentaries viewed as well as to offer additional expectations to foster individual and group accountability.

Applying the Human Rights-Based Approach to In-Country Activities

Once the group arrives in the host country and after the basic safety and health orientation, it is important to assist participants with acclimating to their new environment, including the individuals with whom they will partner. As previously stately, participants' membership in a specific social group (e.g., gender, age, social class, race, religion, sexual orientation, ability, geographic location) can either enhance and/or hinder the intercultural interactions with individuals. However, prior to arriving in-country, participants have critically reflected upon the conscious and unconscious messages about nondominant groups that are disseminated through individuals, institutions, and societies. This self-reflection that examines the contradictions between our values and our lived experiences is the first step in intentionally introducing participants to social justice advocacy (Koester & Lustig, 2015; Spencer, 2008). Next, participants engage in intercultural interactions, participating in dialogue with members from the host country, which fosters and promotes global citizenship (Deardorff, 2009). Consequently, social justice advocacy is realized when individuals, those oppressed and those not oppressed, work cooperatively and take action to eliminate oppression (Spencer, 2008), which occurs during the collaborative participation in the service project that has been identified and is led by members of the host country. Below are activities to apply when in-country. Table 2.3 shows the connection to study abroad educational goals and the human rights-based key concepts.

Cultural Immersion Cultural immersion is providing opportunities for individuals to have experiences that offer direct, prolonged, in vivo contact while immersed in a culture other than their own (Pope-Davis & Coleman, 1997). Harrowing et al. (2012) recognize that even time-limited exposure to individuals from a different culture can result in immediate acquisition of cultural knowledge and skills, being transformative for the participant in their journey to cultural competence. The goal of cultural immersion is to ensure direct contact with individuals whose culture differs from one's own. This is consistent with Allport's (1954) contact theory, which highlights how direct contact with others heightens awareness and reduces misunderstandings and tensions.

Table 2.3 In-country activities within a human rights-based framework

Educational goal	Activity	Key concept
Challenge assumptions Increase awareness Raise critical consciousness Develop cultural humility Foster global citizenship	Cultural immersion	Human dignity Nondiscrimination Participation
Challenge assumptions Increase awareness Raise critical consciousness Develop cultural humility Foster global citizenship	In-country learning	Human dignity Nondiscrimination Participation Transparency Accountability
Challenge assumptions Raise critical consciousness Develop cultural humility Foster global citizenship	Debriefs and critical reflection journal	Human dignity Nondiscrimination Transparency Accountability

These meaningful relationships with host country members challenge participants' biases and foster personal and professional growth, specifically in cultural understanding and empathy (Barden & Cashwell, 2013). This reinforces the human rights-based approach's key concepts of human dignity, nondiscrimination, and participation. Mapp and Rice (2018) describe the importance of designing and implementing short-term study abroad trips in collaboration with members of the host country, ensuring all aspects of the trip (e.g., lodging, meals, activities, service) are carried out in collaboration with and alongside members of the host country.

The trip components need to be formal (e.g., planned visits to agencies, universities, and historical sites) and informal (e.g., eating at local restaurants, shopping at local markets, and participating in local recreational activities). Together they provide participants exposure to the richness of the culture, such as language, traditions, and practices. These cultural immersion experiences promote a sense of global connection that transcends language and cultural barriers and increases a sense of self-efficacy and personal agency (Tomlinson-Clarke & Clarke, 2010). The most critical aspect of cultural immersion is the frequent and direct interactions with community members as it enables participants to experience the daily demands of living with the sociocultural context of another group (Harrowing et al., 2012), which often occurs during informal activities.

For example, hosts of our trip to Nicaragua planned for us to stay at a family-run local hotel where we enjoyed breakfast each morning cooked by their chef. For lunch, we ate either a packed lunch prepared by the hotel's chef or a meal at a local restaurant. To further foster authentic cultural immersion and relationships, one evening, we enjoyed dinner in the homes of our hosts. To facilitate participation, we supplied the ingredients, and the hosts taught us how to make traditional dishes. This immersion experience not only challenges assumptions and raises awareness about another culture but fosters cultural humility and global citizenship.

Cultural immersion through a human rights-based framework positions power with members of the host country. They guide and lead the formal and informal learning that occurs during short-term study abroad trips. The host country members should take the lead in the development of the itinerary and selecting the formal and informal activities. It is also highly recommended that the trip include an activity on the first day of the trip that allows participants to engage with members of the host country to assist with overcoming any barriers to cross-cultural communication. This activity could be a shared meal, recreational activity, or language lesson. Wesp and Baumann (2012) developed a scavenger hunt activity that students on a short-term study abroad trip completed throughout their stay in country. The scavenger hunt was developed by members of the host country to provide students with opportunities to learn about such things as the country's historical challenges, language, and food. The unique feature of the scavenger hunt is that the students had to obtain the answers by asking local residents for the information. What Wesp and Baumann discovered is that beyond discovering factual information about the culture, the students reported the scavenger hunt activity eased the initiation of conversation and increased their appreciation of differences. This is consistent with what Sampson and Jackson (2007) report as ways to increase cultural awareness. In their study, the students who engaged in early, active, and positive experiences had a more positive attitude about other cultures.

We have incorporated this into our planning of our South Africa trip with students. During day one of our trip, our host will lead us on a tour of the neighborhood where we live during our in-country stay. Participants visit and meet local shops and restaurant owners, the local physician, and the local supermarket. This tour offers a guide to where to access essential items and introduces participants to members of the host country, which minimizes culture stress and eases the transition to unfamiliar surroundings.

In-Country Learning In 2009, Schroeder, Wood, Galiardi, and Koehn conducted a study to examine the effect of service trips on host communities. Based on data collected, they concluded that "host communities should have control over if and how student groups should study" (p. 146) to avoid unintended outcomes on local communities. There is a trend to add service work in study abroad programs (Delcambre, 2012); however, in a 2010 study conducted by Nelson, she found there to be many negative effects of volunteer tourism. These negative effects include undermining local control and customs, creating dependency on NGOs by the local people rather than developing capacity to allow for individuals to work actively within their communities, and increasing resentment between community members. Nelson concluded that any trip with an in-country service component should make it a priority to listen to the local community regarding their needs before imposing solutions.

In Chap. 1 of this text, we offered extensive overview of the concerns and challenges of service approached from a position of charity and offered theories to suggest why a collaborative approach such as the human rights-based approach is more beneficial to students, universities, and local communities. It might go without saying, but within a human rights-based framework, all service should work toward the realization of human rights. One way to work toward the realization of human rights is to focus service around action that responds to the challenges framed within the United Nation's Sustainable Development Goals.

In 2016, the United Nations adopted 17 goals that offered an integrated approach to economic and social development, especially driven by the recognition that environmental issues and many health and social challenges know no borders. The Sustainable Development Goals (SDGs) offer a framework for moving toward the realization of meeting the needs of individuals and communities by the 2030 target. By focusing on both the economic and social functioning of individuals and communities, realizing the SDGs requires utilization of a social development model that employs both an integrated family-centered and community-based approach to addressing complex global challenges. Service learning experiences have the potential to teach participants about the structural causes of global poverty and inequality, while also learning techniques and strategies for effective community development. In order to ensure services provided are sustainable and nondiscriminatory, community participation is key as it empowers those affected and fosters social and economic development, which is core to developmental services. A social development model fostering community development aligns with a human rights-based approach to service delivery as there is an aim to minimize power imbalances and foster the importance of collaborative partnerships in response to social challenges (Androff, 2016).

Two examples of how we developed service learning experiences to respond to specific Sustainable Development Goals was a focus on Goal 13: Climate Action in Costa Rica and learning ways members within various communities were making individual and collective changes to reduce their carbon footprint by planting trees, eliminating the use of plastic, and adopting a plant based diet. In South Africa, we focus on the intersection between many of the Sustainable Development Goals (SDG), specifically SDG #1: No Poverty, SDG: #5 Gender Equality, SDG #8: Decent Work and Economic Growth, and SDG #16: Peace, Justice and Strong Institutions. We examine how organizations are utilizing a social development approach to address systemic race and gender inequalities through the promotion of job skills training, employment, and economic justice. Further, these opportunities provide participants with an understanding of how specific NGOs are responding to human rights violations and contributing to positive change.

Debriefs and Critical Reflection Journal A goal of study abroad is to challenge participants to recognize and address internalized biases and assumptions, which hopefully are surfacing as a result of the cultural immersion and in-country learning experiences. For learning to occur, students need to make sense of this new information and process their feelings associated with its meaning (DeRicco & Sciarra, 2005). One way to do this is through regular debriefs as a large group as it supports one another's feelings and individual growth processes. However, offering and encouraging critical self-reflection through journaling is essential because, as previously stated, critical self-reflection is the means through which individuals can create new understanding of situations.

Short-term study abroad that utilizes a human rights-based framework is a start on the cultural competency transformational journey. To foster that transformation, students journal to critically reflect upon their cultural immersion experience and engagement with people whose lives are shaped and structured by complex political, economic, historical, and social forces (Harrowing et al., 2012). Students should be encouraged to critically reflect upon their awareness that colonialization, exploitation, and marginalization contributed to current challenges experienced by members in the host country. Only through this critical examination will students then be able to apply social justice, equity, and relational practices (Harrowing et al., 2012).

Applying the Human Rights-Based Approach to Reentry Activities

Webb (1983) theorized that individuals experience a period of adjustment when reentering their own culture after studying abroad and that the adjustment period forms a W-Curve as individuals will experience a period of honeymoon at home, crisis at home, recovery at home, and adjustment at home (Gullahorn & Gullahorn, 1963). To help explain this adjustment process, research has been conducted on students who have studied abroad. Wielkiewicz and Turkowski (2010) found that upon return, students who studied abroad were more skeptical toward their home culture than students who did not study abroad. This supports other research (e.g., Anderson et al., 2006; Pence & Macgillivray, 2008) that reported psychological changes occur after returning from studying abroad. These psychological challenges range from anxiety, loneliness, isolation, and frustration, to apathy, anger, hostility, helplessness, and even depression (Allison et al., 2011; Chamove & Soeterik, 2006; Walling et al., 2006). Below, we apply a human rights-based approach to reentry activities. These activities and the associated educational goals and human rights-based key concepts are listed on Table 2.4.

Table 2.4 Reentry activities within a human rights-based framework

Educational goal	Activity	Key concept
Raise critical consciousness Develop cultural humility Foster global citizenship	Transformative learning	Human dignity Nondiscrimination Participation Transparency Accountability
Challenge assumptions Increase awareness Raise critical consciousness Develop cultural humility Foster global citizenship	Advocacy and activism	Human dignity Nondiscrimination Participation Transparency Accountability

Transformative Learning Returning home from studying abroad might be challenging both psychologically and socially given participants have engaged in a number of culturally immersive experiences; however, these reentry feelings may be an indicator that participants have become more culturally competent. Kartoshkina (2015) highlighted various explanations (e.g., feeling of loss from international experience ending, inability of family and friends to relate to students' intercultural experiences, changes in cultural identities as a result of studying abroad) as to why participants may find reentry challenging. Therefore, providing opportunities for reentry reflections to unpack the study abroad experience is essential as it allows for further transformative learning to occur.

Transformation often occurs when individuals have an opportunity to grapple with the learning that occurred; reflect upon their changes in knowledge, awareness, and thoughts; and then identify how to continue to challenge their own and others' personal and professional growth related to cultural humility. The first step to continue to foster this personal transformation is to make meaning and develop a deeper understanding of the experiences while abroad (Kindred & Manginelli, n.d.). Barden and Cashwell (2014) suggest encouraging participants to share their experiences and reflections during a debrief with other study abroad participants, family, and friends. Tomlinson-Clarke and Clarke (2010) recommend participating in a culminating event to share experiences with the community and identify how cultural interactions influenced their cultural humility development. Ultimately, the goal is for participants to share their international experiences and share them with others to foster solidarity and promote global citizenship. Some examples of how we assisted our participants in sharing their international experiences with others include speaking to peers during study abroad information sessions, creating a video highlighting the value of studying abroad, and presenting lessons learned during an annual research conference.

Advocacy and Activism The Council on Social Work Education (2015) requires educational, social work programs to provide ample opportunities for students to develop competence related to advocacy and the pursuit of social equity. Healy (2012) reinforces the notion that social workers address global issues on domestic and international levels. As students progress in their transformation related to cultural humility resulting from engaging in immersion and in-country learning while studying abroad, they are better equipped to advocate for social, economic, environmental, and racial justice to realize human rights, domestically and internationally. Taking action further provides participants with an opportunity to reflect on ways the host country responds to human rights violations and to what extent those actions can be applied domestically to promote positive change.

Advocacy is the act of showing support for an organization or cause, while activism is taking direct action to bring about change. Students should be encouraged to advocate for change through direct action. Continued advocacy and activism are a means of reinforcing reciprocity and the relationship between study abroad participants and host members after the study abroad trip ends. It provides an opportunity for participants to continue to support the host community through various advocacy efforts such as fundraising, training, and social development, thus fostering continued accountability of the university to members of the host country. For example, following a study abroad trip to Costa Rica, where the focus of the trip was on realizing environmental justice through waste reduction, reforestation, and community gardening, participants considered ways they could positively effect change within their own communities. Some suggestions included eliminating the use of single use plastic, planting trees, and reducing shower time. Ensuring advocacy approaches utilize a rights-based approach to respond to the global social issues—and our shared involvement in them—promotes social, economic, environmental, and racial justice across all levels of practice and fosters the realization of human rights.

Summary

This chapter highlighted the key concepts of the human rights-based approach to practice: human dignity, nondiscrimination, participation, transparency, and accountability. Applying these key concepts to the pre-departure, in-country, and reentry activities ensures short-term study abroad trips are designed and implemented to promote collaboration between universities and members of the host country in ways that avoid volunteer tourism. In doing so, participants of these human rights-based short-term study abroad trips experience raised critical consciousness through increased cultural awareness and challenged assumptions, increased cultural humility, and fostered global citizenry.

Exercises

Pre-Departure

1. Provide the following prompts to participants asking them to reflect upon them and write responses in a journal that they will return to throughout the trip.
   (a) What are your fears, anticipations, and hopes regarding traveling to this location?
   (b) What can you do, now, to reduce any fears or concerns you might have?
   (c) What can you do within the country to reduce any fears you might have to accomplish your hopes and goals for the trip?
   (d) In regard to your identity, which ones are you most aware and why?
   (e) What do others often assume about you and why?
   (f) What assumptions might you make about individuals with whom we will work as well as the communities in which we will volunteer?

(g) What are the stereotypes that are reinforcing these assumptions?
(h) How might you overcome individual biases to work most effectively with this particular population?
(i) How do you define service and what does service mean to you?
(j) What are specific human rights challenges present within the host country and how has the country responded?

2. As professionals, we must also explore and examine our assumptions and biases (conscious or unconscious). Take any or all of the Implicit Bias assessments at this link (https://implicit.harvard.edu/implicit/education.html), and afterward, consider ways in which you will further enhance your own cultural competency and humility to prevent a "savior" approach to helping.
3. Select articles, movies, documentaries, and/or music videos that offer knowledge about the human rights challenges being addressed and/or will encounter within the country where traveling. These written and visual materials should offer perspectives from various stakeholders. Provide prompts for participants to reflect upon afterward and have them document responses within their critical reflection journal.
4. Host a screening of a documentary that deconstructs a human rights challenge present and/or is relevant to the country where traveling. Afterward, engage in critical dialogue with the participants fostering dialogue that includes both process (feelings) and content (thoughts, application).
5. Have participants engage in various activities to expose them to the culture of the host country. These activities could include eating at authentic ethnic restaurant; practicing the language spoken in host country; and visiting a museum to learn about the people, places, and events of the host country.
6. To expose students to cultural confrontations prior to leaving the country, have individuals choose from any of the following activities and journal about the experience:

   (a) Take a cold shower.
   (b) Turn electricity off for 4 hours during the day.
   (c) Refrain from using cell phone and accessing wi-fi for 24-hour period.
   (d) Only drink bottled water.
   (e) Do not flush toilet paper after use.
   (f) Go without air conditioning for a day during the summer months.

7. To foster global citizenry, host team building activities such as participating in a ropes course, eating together at an ethnic restaurant, visiting a museum, or watching a film and discussing it afterward.
8. During a group gathering (can be coupled with above exercise), have participants write their "Hopes" on one side of an index card and their "Fears" on the other side. Participants should not write their name on the index card. Collect the cards and hand a different card to each participant. Have everyone share aloud the "Fears" listed on the index cards and as they are shared, write them on a large newsprint posted to front of room. Then, do the same for "Hopes."

Afterward, process the similarities and differences. As a group, identify ways to overcome and/or manage the fears, listed. Be sure to discuss the importance of open-mindedness, respect, and dignity and worth of individuals to ensure interactions with members from host country and in-country learning occurs through a human rights-based lens.

9. As a group, during a pre-departure session, develop group expectations and have students list them in their journal that will be taking with them on the trip. Explain that at any time during the trip, anyone can add to the list. Further, explain that the expectations are what we expect of ourselves and others to achieve the trip's learning goals and foster a human rights-based approach to practice.
10. During the pre-departure session, a group identifies ways to prevent perpetuating economic, environmental, and social injustices in the country. Examples might include buying local, using a water bottle, and joining in collaborative service with members of the host country.
11. Host a screening of Poverty, Inc. and discuss the meaning of service, charity, and social development, afterward. Connect the discussion to the mission and goals of your trip and the in-country learning that the participants will do in collaboration with members of the host country. Highlight and connect to key human rights-based concepts such as participation, transparency, and accountability.
12. Research human rights violations and/or abuses present in the host country and relevant international human rights laws (e.g., covenants, treaties). Summarize the country's position on realization of the human right in question.

In-Country

1. Prior to departure, work with members of the host country seeking their assistance in developing a Scavenger Hunt activity that students will carry out throughout the time spent in country. Potential questions and/or activities that students are to answer/complete through their interactions with members of the host country during the formal and informal activities might be related to historical facts about the country, meaning of certain words, a recipe of a country-specific food, and information about country specific traditions.
2. Identify the global issue being addressed by the NGO where service is conducted. Connect the global issue to one or more of the Sustainable Development Goals (SDGs).

   Discuss how the SDG affects the specific community and population targeted by the NGO and how realizing the SDG fosters human rights. Discuss the solution provided by the NGO in order to the address the global issue and what challenges and/or barriers may be preventing full realization of meeting the Global Goals. Identify specific ways to build capacity to empower the local community to respond to the global challenge.

3. Have participants reflect, nightly, and record in their journal responses to these prompts:
   (a) Thoughts and feelings related to what experienced, today.
   (b) Something new learned.
   (c) How did the experiences challenge pre-existing assumptions?
   (d) What human rights are ignored by the host country's government and how might this affect the quality of life of individuals as well as community sustainability?
   (e) How might the new information be applied in home country?
4. Provide participants with relevant websites related to organizations and associations responding to the global issue and human rights, domestically. Ask participants to identify specific actions they can take to promote change.

Reentry

1. Hold a debrief session and have participants share how the study abroad trip affected their prior understanding of the culture visited. Have participants discuss how they can use this new knowledge and perspective to continue to further their own and others' personal and professional growth and knowledge about human rights.
2. Have participants reflect on responses to pre-departure journal prompts and journal how knowledge and/or perspectives have changed as a result of the study abroad experiences. Have participants identify specific cultural immersion experiences that challenged their prior perspectives.
3. One way to stay connected to the culture of the host country visited and continue to foster global citizenship is through our senses. Connecting to others and valuing one another's culture can continue upon return to own country. Encourage participants to engage in any of these activities that connects to our senses and fosters interconnectedness, key attribute related to the human rights-based concept, human dignity.
   (a) Vision: reminisce about the trip by looking through photos from the trip and/or artwork brought back. For those who want to engage, further, encourage participants to draw images from their experiences using any art medium.
   (b) Hearing: listen to the music and sounds of the culture.
   (c) Taste: find a restaurant that serves food enjoyed in the country or enjoy the food items brought back. Those who enjoy cooking encourage participants to find a recipe for the food from the country and make it for themselves, family and friends.
   (d) Touch: wear the clothing and jewelry or use other items such as blankets, pillows, scarves purchased to stay physically connected to the country.

(e) Smell: enjoy the scents of the items (e.g., candles, spices, food) brought home and/or practice imagery and close your eyes and "take yourself" to any place in the country visited to "smell" the scents of the area.

Provide participants with relevant websites related to organizations and associations responding to the global issue and human rights, domestically. Ask participants to identify specific actions they can take to promote change.

References

Adler, P. (1977). Beyond cultural identity: Reflections upon cultural and multicultural man. In *Culture learning: Concepts, applications and research.* University Press of Hawaii.

Allison, P., Davis-Berman, J., & Berman, D. (2011). Changes in latitude, changes in attitude: Analysis of the effects of reverse culture shock – A study of students returning from youth expeditions. *Leisure Studies, 30*, 1–17.

Allport, G. W. (1954). *The nature of prejudice*. Addison-Wesley.

Anderson, P. H., Lawton, L., Rexeisen, R. J., & Hubbard, A. C. (2006). Short-term study abroad and intercultural sensitivity: A pilot study. *International Journal of Intercultural Relations, 30*, 457–469.

Androff, D. (2016). *Practicing rights: Human rights-based approaches to social work practice.* Taylor & Francis Group.

Barden, S. M., & Cashwell, C. S. (2013). Critical factors in cultural immersion: A synthesis of relevant literature. *International Journal for the Advancement of Counselling, 35*, 286–297.

Barden, S. M., & Cashwell, C. S. (2014). International immersion in counselor education: A consensual qualitative research investigation. *Faculty Bibliography, 42*, 5027. Retrieved from: https://stars.library.ucf.edu/facultybib2010/5027 p 41-60

Bennet, J. M. (2002). NAFSA trainer corps presentation handout. San Antonio, Texas.

Berk, R. A. (2009). Multimedia teaching with video clips: TV, movies, YouTube, and mtvU in the college classroom. *International Journal of Technology in Teach and Learning, 5*, 1–21.

Blau, P. (1964). *Exchange and power in social life*. John Wiley & Sons.

Brown, J. (2001). L1 attrition among native-speakers of English resident abroad: A sociolinguistic case-study from Foggia, Italy. Unpublished MA Linguistics (TESOL). University of Surrey.

Chamove, A. S., & Soeterik, S. M. (2006). Grief in returning sojourners. *Journal of Social Sciences, 13*, 215–220.

Corbett, S., & Fikkert, B. (2012). *When helping hurts: How to alleviate poverty without hurting the poor . . . and yourself.* Moody Publishers.

Council on Social Work Education. (2015). *Educational policy and accreditation standards*. Author.

Dantas, M. L. (2007). Building teacher competency to work with diverse learners in the context of international education. *Teacher Education Quarterly, 34*, 75–95.

Deardorff, D. K. (2009). *The SAGE handbook of intercultural competence*. Sage Publications, Inc.

Delcambre, S. J. (2012). Community perspectives – How study abroad with service learning impacts the locals. *Capstone Collection,* 2543. Retrieved from: https://digitalcollections.sit.edu/capstones/2543

DeRicco, J. N., & Sciarra, D. T. (2005). The immersion experience in multicultural counselor training: Confronting covert racism. *Journal of Multicultural Counseling and Development, 33*, 2–16.

Dutko, M. (2016). I matter, as does the world: Critical consciousness in higher education. *Dissertations*, 182. https://digitalcommons.nl.edu/diss/182

Fisher, C. M., & Grettenberger, S. E. (2015). Community-based participatory study abroad: A proposed model for social work education. *Journal of Social Work Education, 51*, 566–582.

Foucault, M. (1980). *Power/knowledge: Selected interviews and other writings*. Pantheon Books.
Freire, P. (1970). *Pedagogy of the oppressed*. Continuum.
Gatenio Gabel, S. (2015). Foreword. In K. R. Libal & S. Harding (Eds.), *Human rights-based community practice in the United States* (pp. v–xv). Springer.
Gullahorn, J. T., & Gullahorn, J. E. (1963). An extension of the U-curve hypothesis. *Journal of Social Issues, 19*, 33–47.
GundyKunst, W. G. (2003). *Cross-cultural and intercultural communication*. Sage.
Harrowing, J. N., Gregory, D. M., O'Sullivan, P. S., Lee, B., & Doolittle, L. (2012). A critical analysis of undergraduate students' cultural immersion experiences. *International Nurses Review, 12*, 494–501.
Hartman, E., & Kiely, R. (2014). A critical global citizenship. In M. Johnson & P. M. Green (Eds.), *Crossing boundaries: Tension and transformation in international service- learning* (pp. 215–242). Stylus.
Healy, L. M. (2012). Defining international social work. In L. M. Healy & R. J. Link (Eds.), *Handbook of international social work: Human rights, development, and the global profession* (pp. 9–15). Oxford University Press.
Hooks, B., & Sealey, K. S. (2001). On the topic of film and education: A conversation with bell hooks. *Film, politics, and education: Cinematic pedagogy across the disciplines. Afterward.* New York: Peter Lang.
Kartoshkina, Y. (2015). Bitter-sweet reentry after studying abroad. *International Journal of Intercultural Relations, 44*, 35–45.
Kindred, C., & Manginelli, A. (n.d.). *Making meaning of education abroad: A journal for the returnee experience*. NAFSA.
Koester, J., & Lustig, M. W. (2015). Intercultural communication competence: Theory, measurement, and application. *International Journal of Intercultural Relations, 48*, 20–31.
Mapp, S., & Rice, K. (2018). Conducting rights-based short-term study abroad experiences. *Social Work Education, 38*, 427–438.
Marcus, A. S., & Stoddard, J. D. (2009). The inconvenient truth about teaching history with documentary film: Strategies for presenting multiple perspectives and controversial issues. *The Social Studies, 33*, 279–284.
McPherson, J. (2015). Human rights practice in social work: A rights-based framework & two new measures (Doctoral dissertation). Retrieved from ProQuest Dissertations and Theses (Accession Order No. AAT 3705877).
Mitchell, R. (2015). The development of social relations during residence abroad. *Innovation in Language Learning and Teaching, 9*(1), 22–33.
NAFSA: Association of International Educators. (2015). *Trends in U.S. study abroad.*
National Association of Social Workers. (2017). *Code of ethics*. Author.
Nelson, E. (2010). A community perspective on volunteer tourism and development in South Africa. (unpublished thesis). Miami, FL: Miami University.
Pence, H. M., & Macgillivray, I. K. (2008). The impact of an international field experience on preservice teachers. *Teaching and Teacher Education, 24*, 14–25.
Pope-Davis, D. B., & Coleman, H. L. (1997). *Multicultural counseling competencies: Assessment, education, and training, and supervision*. Sage.
Ross, L. (2010). Notes from the field: Learning cultural humility through critical incidents and central challenges in community-based participatory research. *Journal of Community Practice, 18*, 315–335.
Rotabi, K. S., Roby, J., & Bunkers, K. (2017). Altruistic exploitation: Orphan tourism and global social work. *British Journal of Social Work, 47*(3), 648–665.
Sampson, D. C., & Jackson, M. J. (2007). Armchair travel: An interactive learning approach to increasing global awareness and participant self-efficacy. *Developments in Business Simulations and Experiential Learning, 34*, 374–378.
Schroeder, K., Wood, C., Galiardi, S., & Koehn, J. (2009). First, do no harm: Ideas for mitigating negative community impacts of short term study abroad. *Journal of Geography, 108*, 141–147.

Schuessler, J. B., Wilder, B., & Byrd, L. W. (2012). Reflective journaling and development of cultural humility in students. *Nursing Education Perspectives, 33*, 96–99.

Spencer, M. (2008). A social worker's reflections on power, privilege and oppression. *Social Work, 53*, 99–101.

Summerfield, E., Sibley, A., & Stellmaker, H. (1997). Predeparture orientation and reentry programming. In W. Hoffa & J. Pearson (Eds.), *NAFSA's guide to education abroad for advisers and administrators* (pp. 233–253). Washington, DC: NAFSA.

Tomlinson-Clarke, S. M., & Clarke, D. (2010). Culturally focused community-centered service learning: An international cultural immersion experience. *Journal of Multicultural Counseling & Development, 38*, 166–175.

United Nations. (1948). Universal declaration of human rights.

United Nations. (2016). *Sustainable development goals*. Retrieved from:https://sdgs.un.org/goals.

United Nations High Commissioner for Human Rights. (2006). *Frequently asked questions on a human rights-based approach to development cooperation*. Retrieved from https://www.ohchr.org/Documents/Publications/FAQen.pdf

Walling, S. M., Eriksson, C. B., Meese, K. J., Ciovica, A., & Gorton, D. (2006). Cultural identity and reentry in short-term student missionaries. *Journal of Psychology and Theology, 34*, 153–164.

Watts, R. J., Abdul-Adil, J. K., & Pratt, T. (2002). Enhancing critical consciousness in young African American men: A psychoeducational approach. *Psychology of Men and Masculinity, 3*, 41–50.

Webb, M. W. (1983). Cross-cultural awareness: A framework for interaction. *Personnel and Guidance Journal, 61*, 498–500.

Wesp, R., & Baumann, A. (2012). A cultural scavenger hunt: Tools of engagement. *Psychology and Teaching, 11*, 423–427.

Wielkiewicz, R. M., & Turkowski, L. W. (2010). Reentry issues upon returning from study abroad programs. *Journal of College Student Development, 51*, 649–664.

Wronka, J. M. (2008). *Human rights and social justice: Social action and service for the helping and health professions*. Sage.

Chapter 3
Evidence of Effects of Human Rights-Based Short-Term Study Abroad

Since 2013, we have organized 14 short-term study abroad trips to six different countries/territories. The countries visited were intentional and dependent upon the relationships already established by our study abroad partners, who have spent years cultivating authentic, meaningful relationships with NGOs collaborating with members of their communities to respond to identified challenges. These partners utilize a study abroad framework that aligns with the human rights-based approach. The itinerary and in-country learning related to addressing one or more of the Sustainable Development Goals are community-driven and always done in collaboration with members of the host country (see Table 3.1). Further, the itineraries are created to provide participants with formal and informal learning opportunities to raise awareness, examine assumptions, foster cultural humility, and develop global citizenry.

Across the 14 short-term study abroad trips we organized, 146 individuals participated. Within 3 months post-return from the trip, participants were sent an email asking them to voluntarily complete a survey of their perceptions of the various aspects of the short-term study abroad trip that most affected their personal and professional growth. The survey allows trip developers to ascertain which formal and/or informal aspects of the trip led to the growth. To determine if participation in short-term study abroad trips developed utilizing a human rights-based framework affect participants' advocacy and/or activism upon return from the trip, participants are asked to describe how they will apply the human rights-based framework they learned to advocacy.

We carried out such a survey and report the findings within each of the three areas assessed that at least 50% of the participants identified. Within each area, three themes emerged.

K. Rice, H. Girvin, *Human Rights-Based Approach to Short-Term Study Abroad*, SpringerBriefs in Rights-Based Approaches to Social Work, https://doi.org/10.1007/978-3-030-87421-6_3

Table 3.1 Sample in-country learning focus

Working partners	Country	SDGs: Focus of in-country learning
VACorps	South Africa	SDG 1: No poverty SDG 16: Peace, justice, and strong institutions
SOL Education	Costa Rica Nicaragua Mexico	SDG 5: Gender equality SDG 12: Responsible consumption and production SDG 13: Climate action SDG 15: Life on land SDG 4: Quality education
Amizade	Northern Ireland Puerto Rico	SDG 10: Reduced inequalities SDG 13: Climate action

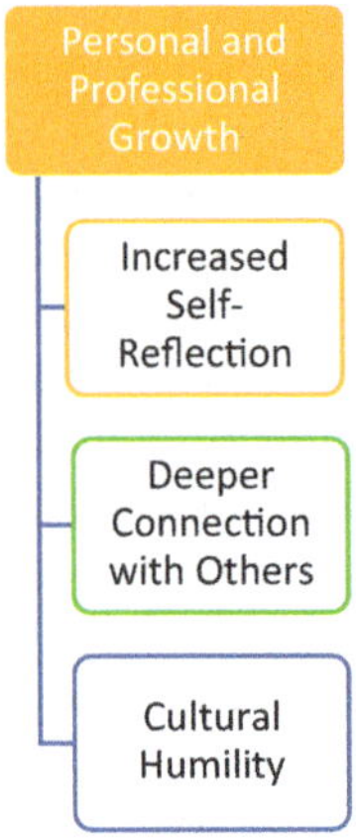

Fig. 3.1 Effect of short-term study abroad trips on personal and professional growth

Personal and Professional Growth Outcomes

Participants were asked to identify how their participation in the short-term study abroad trip affected them. The three themes that emerged following analysis of the data were increased self-reflection, deeper connection with others, and cultural humility (Fig. 3.1). Each area will be further examined.

Increased Self-Reflection The majority of the participants recognized the transformation related to their own perceptions and behaviors due to the "eye-opening" experience. Participants recognized being more aware of their own privilege and "humbled to know that I do not need everything that I have to be happy." There was more assessment of what one has and needs but also of individual situations and how they typically responded. Participants reported that they now focus more on the "positives" of a situation rather than on the "problem" or "what went wrong." Further, they report not being "as judgmental and think more thoughtfully about different interactions." This reflection led to being more "open-minded" and recognition that "everyone has a story and cannot make broad sweeping statements to characterize and label an entire country."

Deeper Connection with Others Participants spoke of the increased compassion they developed toward others, both within the host country and those with whom they traveled. "Living with strangers for two weeks challenged me to be less introverted" and "deepened my care for and dependence upon others." Participants described the relationships and "lifelong friendships" they developed with members from the host country. As one participant stated, the "unfamiliar can become comfortable and relationships are the way to positive change."

Cultural Humility Participants spoke of "giving up" ways of thinking, doing, and seeing situations and having a "love for another country." They recognized that "different is not wrong, just another way of living." This "difference" was in both how they perceived individuals but also how they believed practice ought to be implemented. As one participant stated, they were "able to look beyond person's situation and see person, first." Further, "regardless of differences or where live, we can support and lift up others." As for expanding perceptions around ways of practice, participants acknowledged that there is no one right way to doing something and that the trip afforded them "more confidence in how to advocate in a collaborative way." One participant stated, "as a nurse practitioner in the US, I had to learn to give up what knew and open self to experiences in front of me to grow and learn and be better nurse and person." This personal growth in recognizing additional ways to practice was echoed by the majority of the participants as participants realized the "American way is not the only way," and that the "US can learn a lot from other countries."

Program Components Contributing to Growth

As a result of participating in the short-term study abroad trip, participants were asked to identify the specific aspects of the program that contributed to their learning. The three themes that emerged were engaging in learning opportunities, hearing personal stories, and participating in collaborative service (Fig. 3.2). This is further explored, below.

Engaging in Learning Opportunities From the beginning, prior to traveling to the country, participants identified how the pre-departure activities such as learning about the history of the country (e.g., apartheid in South Africa, Troubles in Northern Ireland, the United States and Puerto Rico relationship, and Mexico/US border issues) broadened their perspectives and understanding of current situations. "I understand current challenges in the country are related to past relations with the US." Once in country, participants identified appreciating experiencing new foods, dance, music, and language. Participants further identified appreciating learning about and visiting the various services available within the host country to meet the needs of the community. "I enjoyed learning about how the environment, specifically the mangroves were important to the region to prevent flooding." Through

Fig. 3.2 Aspects of short-term study abroad contributing to growth

these formal and informal learning activities, participants were able to "see the similarities and differences in programming, services, living, and lifestyle." These learning activities also illuminated challenges that might exist such as "lack of access to services and resources in rural areas of the country."

Hearing Personal Stories Although participants recognized the importance of the formal and informal activities in positively affecting their learning, they highlighted the value of hearing another person's story. Being "able to view situations from those experiencing it and learn from them offer new perspective and appreciation for the experience." Listening to others and hearing their stories provided participants with "context for why risk life to migrate to the US" and "learn truth about the recovery efforts and how being ignored by US government." In addition to learning firsthand from those who experienced a situation to offer another perspective on how it affects those within the host country, participants recognized hearing personal stories challenged their own assumptions. "Hearing personal stories have challenged me to examine own assumptions and see world differently."

Participating in Collaborative Service All participants recognized the value of working collaboratively with individuals within the host country as "able to learn from community," and the service being completed is "done as a team to benefit" members of the host country. Further, participants highlighted that "working alongside" members within the community "offered insight into new ways to communicate when don't share same language." It was clear that service done collaboratively and alongside members of the community offered our participants an opportunity to "learn from the locals" but also challenged their perceptions about how service should be done. "Community driven change and projects are far more effective than outside driven."

Continued Transformation as Global Citizens

The third and final question asked on the survey was what specific action steps participants took since return from the short-term study abroad trip that promotes social, economic, environmental, and/or racial justice. Engaging in just actions contribute to the realization of human rights and exemplifies an aspect of global citizenry, an outcome to a human rights-based approach to practice. The three main themes that emerged were volunteer, education, and attitude and behavior changes (Fig. 3.3).

Volunteer Participants reported ways they engaged their own communities through "donations to organizations," "volunteer with local NPOs," and "support of African community within my area." One participant was "using Spanish speaking skills to assist youth in preschools who are English learners." Other ways participants volunteered were through joining advisory boards "to advocate for folks with developmental disorders" or engaging in political advocacy to "help others get registered to vote" or "help certain people get elected."

Education Participants identified a number of activities to continue their education and enhance their knowledge and skills. These included "understanding more how government works and how it affects others," "participating in an internship in the local community to improve medical care provided to others," and "traveling more to keep learning." Others reported changing their major or focus of studies to one that will allow them to help others or have a positive effect on a specific population (e.g., nursing, international studies, immigrants) or joining the Peace Corps. In addition to identifying ways they continued their learning, participants highlighted how they are contributing to the education of others by "raise awareness through social media" and "pass what learned onto own children so they are compassionate."

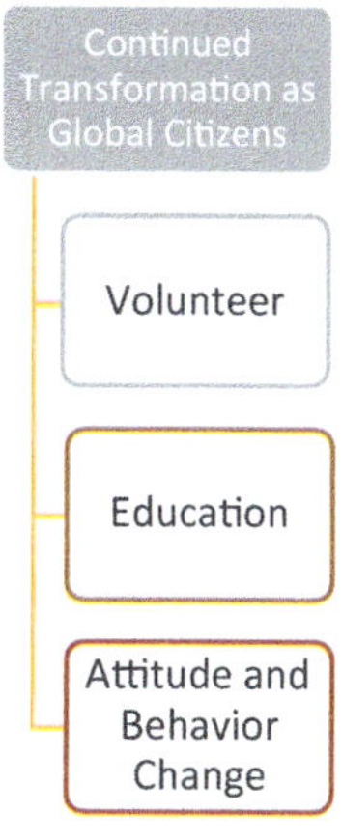

Fig. 3.3 Action related to continued transformation as global citizens

Attitude and Behavior Changes Participants highlighted both attitude and behavior changes as a result of participating in the short-term study abroad trip. Attitudinally, participants recognized that they "practice with humility" within their profession and are "more empathetic." For example, one participant shared that their practice with individuals who experience violence was enhanced as they "get to know them and their story," first. In addition to the changes in attitude, participants recognized that they also changed their behaviors due to their participation in the short-term study abroad trip. These behavioral changes altered personal behaviors to promote sustainability and reduce the negative effect on the environment, such as "use metal straws," "limit shower time," and "started a garden to reduce food waste."

Connection to Findings in the Literature

The results from our study show that participants of our short-term study abroad trips designed utilizing a human rights-based framework experienced personal and professional growth and transformation as a global citizen due to engaging in specific formal and informal activities and collaborative service. These short-term experiences produced transformation by challenging assumptions, increasing awareness, raising critical consciousness, developing cultural humility, and fostering global citizenship. As one student summed it up, "you cannot learn this much information about a community or people from just reading about it. Traveling to, working side by side, and spending time with the people from communities allows us to truly learn."

A number of researchers have examined the effects of study abroad trips, related explicitly to student changes. Similar to our findings, they also found students became more globally minded, acquired new knowledge, and developed personally. For example, Donitsa-Schmidt and Vadish (2015) assessed students' attitude and knowledge following a study abroad trip to Israel. Participants reported an increased positive attitude toward the Hebrew language and Israeli culture. Further, their knowledge of Judaism and Israeli politics and current affairs improved post-trip. Learning about the culture and current affairs in Israel was part of this trip's predeparture preparation. Engle and Crowne (2014) also engaged students in predeparture activities, including reading articles and watching films about the history of the Latin American countries the students were visiting.

Engle and Crowne (2014) studied over 130 college students assessing the extent to which a short-term (1 to 2 weeks) study abroad trip positively affected cultural intelligence. In addition to the pre-departure activities, Engle and Crowne utilized Allport's (1954) contact theory as their guide. They ensured the students had multiple opportunities to engage with members of the host country. Compared to students who did not participate in this study abroad trip, participants reported higher levels of adjustment to new situations when given the opportunity to engage in close contact with members of the host country. Cubillos and Ilvento (2013) also found that students who studied abroad and reported interactions with members of the host country (e.g., shopping at local markets, attending worship services, visiting with individuals within their homes) had higher levels of self-efficacy in academic performance upon return from the trip. Therefore, it is not surprising that our participants identified collaborative service as a benefit to their learning. This aligns with findings from other researchers, which highlighted the benefits of engaging in close contact with members of another culture. The human rights-based framework supports participation with members from the host country, but the manner in which it is implemented is vital. For our short-term study abroad trips, we ensure that all participation is community-driven and collaborative with members of the host country leading the learning and service implemented. This ensures authentic contact as it eliminates power imbalances, essential in the development of cultural humility.

The majority of the studies examined focused on the transformation that occurs in early, formative years of the college experience (sophomore to junior year) as well as on the academic learning (e.g., language acquisition, self-efficacy) rather than ongoing and long-term effect (e.g., cultural humility, global citizenry) that short-term study abroad programs have on participants as our study examined and which the human rights-based framework aims to impact (see, Table 3.2). One study that did examine the long-term global engagement of students who participated in study abroad while in college was conducted by Paige et al. (2009).

Paige et al. (2009) surveyed over 6000 past study abroad participants across 22 different institutions of higher education. Utilizing a scale they developed, Global Engagement Survey, Paige and colleagues assessed the extent to which participants perceived their study abroad experience influenced their global engagement at least 6 years post their study abroad experience. The majority of the respondents considered the study abroad trip as their most impactful college experience.

Eighty-five percent of the participants spent a minimum of 1 month in the country with over half spending 3 to 4 months studying abroad (Paige et al., 2009). The participants of this study were asked to identify the specific global engagement activities they participated in because of their study abroad experience. The global engagement activities included civic engagement (e.g., voting, socially conscious purchases), knowledge production (e.g., obtaining an advanced degree, informed career path), voluntary simplicity (e.g., lead more modest, simpler life), philanthropy (e.g., volunteer work, donations), and social entrepreneurship (e.g., influence NPOs and/or organizations from within). Over half of the participants reported their global engagement activities were to a large or some degree, due to their study abroad experience. This study is significant as it explored the long-term effect of the study abroad experience on participant's likelihood to take action, a key component of global citizenry. However, almost all the participants engaged in a traditional study abroad experience lasting a full semester. With the increase in short-term study abroad experiences coupled with an in-country learning component, it is essential to ensure the design of these trips offer the same outcomes, or the intended effect of this high impact practice is not fully realized.

Table 3.2 Comparison of study abroad participant short-term and long-term outcomes

Research study	Short-term	Long-term
Cubillos and Ilvento (2013)	Increased self-efficacy in academics	
Donitsa-Schmidt and Vadish (2015)	Globally minded Knowledge attainment Positive attitude change	
Engle and Crowne (2014)	Increased cultural intelligence	
Paige et al. (2009)		Increased global engagement Civic engagement. Knowledge production. Voluntary simplicity. Philanthropy. Social entrepreneurship.
Rice and Girvin (outlined above)	Increased self-reflection Deeper connection with others Increased cultural humility	Volunteerism Further knowledge attainment Attitude and behavioral changes

Future Research Considerations

All short-term study abroad trips should include an evaluation of its outcomes to assess the extent to which it not only meets the educational outcomes but challenges assumptions, increases awareness, raises critical consciousness, develops cultural humility, and fosters global citizenship. The methodology employed can be qualitative, quantitative, or mixed methods. There are a few scales including the Global Engagement Survey developed by Paige et al. (2009) that can assess specific outcome components. Additional scales to consider are the Human Rights Engagement in Social Work (HRESW) and Human Rights Exposure in Social Work (HRXSW) to measure participants engagement in and exposure to human rights (McPherson & Abell, 2012).

Further areas of assessment should include the trip leader and members of the host country. It is essential for trip leaders also to assess our own assumptions and biases to avoid modeling behaviors not aligned with the human rights-based framework. In Chap. 1, we suggest completing implicit bias surveys as one approach. Post trip, it is always beneficial to reflect on what went well and what would do differently to ensure better alignment with key components of the human rights-based approach to maximize participant outcomes.

Another area to assess of any short-term study abroad trip is the perception of members of the host country on the perceived benefits and challenges as well as suggested changes. Utilizing a human rights-based approach to designing and implementing short-term study abroad trips should mitigate potential harm to host countries; however, to know for sure, assessing the economic, environmental, and sociocultural impact is essential as these are the main ways in which study abroad programs can negatively affect host communities (Malfatti & Donovan White, 2018).

Seeking feedback from members of the host country also fosters accountability, ensures full participation by members of the host country in all aspects of the study abroad experience, and supports ongoing respect for the dignity and worth of individuals with whom you partnered, key concepts of a human rights-based approach to practice. Sharing summary assessment of post-trip evaluation results with all participants and members of the host country fosters transparency and accountability and ensures future trips are designed to consider necessary changes based on the evaluation results.

Summary

As we know, acquiring cultural humility is not an end state but rather an ongoing process of constant evaluation of personal assumptions compared to information gleaned from firsthand narratives, direct observations and participation, and formal education. Utilizing a human rights-based framework to developing and implementing short-term study abroad trips ensures a continued state of self-reflection that challenges assumptions, raises awareness, increases critical consciousness, fosters cultural humility, and develops global citizenry. Therefore, a human rights-based framework will lead to immediate outcomes (e.g., increased knowledge about the history of the country, increased empathy toward members of the host country) but also the long-term impact that reaches beyond specific members of a host country and extends to others experiencing injustices (e.g., engaging in political advocacy, volunteering at local NPOs, changing personal and others' behaviors to effect change positively) as participants learn a way of examining human rights violations and ways to respond to them as they now understand their role in fostering positive social change.

Findings from data collected from our participants demonstrated varied and broad positive outcomes as perceived by individuals when trips were structured utilizing a human rights-based framework. These outcomes were consistent with findings in previous research, but no prior research studies were found that examined personal and professional growth as well as ongoing transformation outcomes upon trip return as a result of the way in which the trip was designed. If a benefit of study abroad is to increase self-awareness and promote global citizenship, then we need to ensure that all study abroad experiences, especially short-term study abroad trips, given the increase in their interest, are designed in a way that ensures these outcomes and further promotes participants' ongoing cultural humility and global citizenry transformation.

Short-term study abroad experiences have the opportunity to raise critical consciousness about the human rights violations perpetrated worldwide and assist participants in identifying their role in fostering social, economic, environmental, and racial justice, key components of global citizenry. The key to developing these skills within study abroad participants is the manner in which short-term study abroad trips are designed. If not done thoughtfully, then trip leaders may unintentionally cause more harm than good and perpetuate the exact elements they wish to mitigate (e.g., ethnocentrism, exploitation, and environmental damage).

Exercises

1. Identify an existing scale that measures any expected study abroad outcome and examine the extent to which it assesses key components of the human rights-based framework.
2. Develop an evaluation plan for your own short-term study abroad trip that seeks feedback from trip participants, members from host country, and self/trip leaders. Be sure the evaluation plan assesses human rights knowledge and application, short/immediate outcomes, and long-term impact goals.
3. Utilizing skills and knowledge gleaned from global experiences, develop a plan that mitigates the economic, environmental, and sociocultural impact of human behavior within your own communities.

References

Allport, G. W. (1954). *The nature of prejudice*. Perseus Book Group.

Cubillos, J. H., & Ilvento, T. (2013). The impact of study abroad on students' self-efficacy perceptions. *Foreign Language Annals, 45*, 494–511.

Donitsa-Schmidt, S., & Vadish, M. (2015). North American students in Israel: An evaluation of a study abroad experience. *The Forum on Education Abroad,11*, 33–56.

Engle, R., & Crowne, K. A. (2014). The impact of international experience on cultural intelligence: An application of contact theory in a structured short-term program. *Human Resource Development International, 17*, 30–46.

Malfatti, G., & Donovan White, C. (2018). Fostering positive engagement between students and host communities. *International Educator, May/June*, 40–42.

McPherson, J., & Abell, N. (2012). Human rights engagement and exposure: New scales to challenge social work education. *Research on Social Work Practice, 22*, 704–713.

Paige, R. M., Fry, G. W., Stallman, E. M., Josić, J., & Jon, J. E. (2009). Study abroad for global\ engagement: The long-term impact of mobility experiences. *Intercultural Education, 20*(sup1), S29–S44.

Chapter 4
Utility of the Human Rights-Based Approach

The social work profession maintains a storied history of helping the oppressed, righting wrongs, and speaking for those denied opportunities or platforms to speak for themselves. Our dedication to helping others has remained, but, over the years, our strategies for "helping" have not kept pace with the reality that well-intended efforts can quite easily fall short, be derailed by mission creep, or simply be poorly informed. Worse, well-intended help that is shaped by these pitfalls can entrench the status quo, fortifying the distance between "helpers" and "helped," and leave communities who sought support feeling betrayed.

The social work profession is rooted in advocacy, social justice, and human rights. Short-term trips abroad have become a valued method of educating social work students while aligning with our mission. At least, that is the intent. In service of these dual objectives, short-term study abroad trips must be guided by efforts to help empower community members rather than provide charity that fosters dependence, reinforces status differentials, and makes authentic collaboration unlikely. We offer the human rights-based approach to service-learning as a strategy that aligns with ideals of social work education, serves the higher objective of social justice, and preserves professional integrity. As we note in Chap. 2, by following this framework, we replace our habit of "helping" with a commitment to joining in solidarity to seek social justice.

As outlined in this book, the human rights-based approach has proven to be an invaluable pedagogical framework. It has been utilized successfully to maximize ethical service and learn in the short-term study abroad trips that have become an essential part of social work field education. Its learning structure is immersive. Consider, for example, full semesters abroad, half- or year-long international field experiences. The pillars of the human rights-based framework remain solid anchors for student learning. Given an extended timeline, students may feel more immersed in cultures and experiences offered by partner communities. The longer timeline allows for deeper relationships (and therefore true and balanced reciprocity), critical

K. Rice, H. Girvin, *Human Rights-Based Approach to Short-Term Study Abroad*, SpringerBriefs in Rights-Based Approaches to Social Work,
https://doi.org/10.1007/978-3-030-87421-6_4

cognitive processing (that challenges stereotypes "helpers" may bring with them), and opportunities to develop longer-term plans, with transparency and guidelines to create and assess accountability. Of equal importance is the relationship between the human rights-based approach and social justice. The framework offers students a deep, experiential approach to understanding not just difference but the ranking of difference that undergirds social and economic injustice globally.

The human rights-based perspective is no less relevant to domestic service opportunities. Contemporary social movements, political unrest, the renewed commitment to exposing structural oppression, and the pandemic of COVID-19 have created a moment in time that is rich with the capacity for profound and lasting change. Contemporary conditions can be viewed as a result of our country's failure to engage all humans in the work of creating a democracy that celebrates diversity and equity for all its members. Social work students engaged in domestic service opportunities have a map at hand that can help them chart a new path toward protecting human rights for all Americans.

Moving from the field and back into the classroom, the human rights-based perspective has additional utility, as it could benefit social work education in at least three other ways.

Enhancing the Social Work Curriculum

In 2015, CSWE renewed social work's dedication to its core values by making the profession's dedication to global human rights more explicit. According to CSWE's educational policies, Competency 3 requires social workers to "advance human rights and social, economic, and environmental justice" (CSWE, 2020). To achieve this competency, social workers must demonstrate that they understand that all persons have fundamental rights, such as freedom, safety, privacy, an adequate standard of living, health care, and education (CSWE, 2020). Additionally, competent social workers *pursue* this outcome by "understand[ing] strategies designed to eliminate oppressive structural barriers to ensure that social goods, rights, and responsibilities are distributed equally, and that civil, political, environmental, economic, social, and cultural human rights are protected" (CSWE, 2020).

According to the Council on Social Work Education, Competency 3 requires expression *across all social work competencies* (CSWE, 2020). Though this text has highlighted the necessary adoption of the human rights-based framework for short-term study abroad trips, the EPAS remind us that content related directly to human rights—that is, civil, political, environmental, economic, social, and cultural justice—is present in some form across required social work courses in CSWE-accredited programs. For example, electives address populations are directly affected by unjust policies and structures, while "practice courses" teach strategies that target micro-, mezzo-, and macro-points of intervention. Human Behavior in the Social Environment courses explain the dynamic interplay between human action and the structures that shape it, while courses on diversity teach that each person's experience of those structures may differ according to ethnicity or privilege.

As social work educators, our tasks include not only creating curricula that embrace a human rights-based perspective during short-term study abroad trips but constructing classroom content that expresses this same framework across competencies and courses.

Parallel Pedagogy

In the introduction of this text, we discuss the strengths-based perspective, which so profoundly affected social work practice. An interesting facet of this perspective's integration into the social work profession is that the approach infused practice and, eventually, the education of social work students, as well. Over 20 years ago, Hurd (1998) advocated for the incorporation of principles of strengths-based social work into social work education. According to Hurd, this strengths-based pedagogy focused on the interactions of educators with students and allowed educators to instill content and practice competence, while simultaneously instilling a *sense of competence in students*. In this early study, Hurd found an overall change in students' perceptions of professional strengths that would equip students with a greater sense of overall preparedness to enter the field.

The strengths-based pedagogy also emerged as a strategy for meeting a challenge faced by many students: academic or professional writing. Kahn and Holody (2009) argued that there is a special relevancy of the strengths-based approach to social work education, as it is embodied in a pedagogy known as Writing Across the Curriculum (WAC). Within this curriculum, Kahn and Holody view the improvement of student writing from a strengths-based lens, advising that educators can and should include students in the language of the profession and develop writing assignments in creative and integrative ways that allow for the instructor's conscious use of self to encourage learning.

In 2010, the authors of this text (Rice & Girvin, 2010) conducted an exploratory study to determine whether a strengths-based pedagogy could change students' typically negative perceptions of child welfare as an area of practice. We found that centering this child welfare course on a strengths-based perspective exerted a positive influence on undergraduate social work students' perception of the parent/caseworker relationship. In 2018, Toros argued that it is essential for social work educators to explore their own pedagogical approaches related to the strengths-based perspective "versus" the deficit-approach that has shaped so much of social work intervention. According to Toros, students' perceptions of their own strengths and weaknesses affect their adoption of core social work values, and educators must be willing to change their own views and teaching methods to prepare future social work professionals.

The key concepts of the strengths-based perspective have shaped the delivery of pedagogy in promising ways. Similarly, the key concepts of the human rights-based approach to practice, as described by Androff (2015), may inform educators' delivery of content in ways that improve education and align with the social work profession's core values. A human rights-based framework, when applied to pedagogy, would require that educators seek and preserve the *human dignity* present in all students. Educators are thus reminded of their responsibility to review critically the content and structure of their courses, removing content or strategies that are inherently racist, sexist, homophobic, or in any way *discriminatory* or demeaning. Educators would build strategies of student engagement, recognizing that student *participation* and collaboration facilitate learning. *Transparency* and *accountability* would structure course syllabi and classroom practices. Grading policies and expectations would be clear. Educators would deliver appropriate content that illuminates the competencies related to their courses, infusing justice and human rights-based content throughout. Students would be equally supported in their diverse learning needs.

A Generalized Approach to Service and Learning

Beyond social work service trips abroad, domestic service trips, and social work education, the need for a more generalized and widespread promulgation of the human rights-based perspective is apparent. As of this writing, a quick online search with key terms "service abroad trips" produces over 59,000,000 results. If "abroad" is removed from the search, the results are over five times greater. A rudimentary measure at best, yet these results suggest a proliferation of opportunities for people to "serve" in places near to and far from their homes. Religious groups and institutions, of course, have an extensive history of travel and service. Universities and colleges have organized such trips for decades. A more recent development is the emergence of not-for-profit and for-profit agencies that provide various services related to travel, education, and service in communities domestic and global.

A quick review of our country's "service history" (see Chap. 1, for example) should cause us some concern related to the ethics and implications of this new "service industry." Our country's history of service, in its various forms, has been marred by ethnocentrism, wrongheaded objectives, unregulated ideological impulses, and corruption. It may be that sharing the human rights-based framework for domestic and international service endeavors allows our profession to intercede in a way that is ethical, useful, and aligned with our profession's values. Most of our global advocacy and governmental organizations have embraced the human rights-based perspective, applying it to everything from health concerns (e.g., the World Health Organization), to general global policy (e.g., the United Nations), and to global, vulnerable populations, such as women and children (e.g., the United Nations Children's Fund).

Though this text explains the benefit of framing short-term study abroad trips with the human rights-based perspective, its content is not "social work specific." Its broad applicability would allow for its integration into service trips organized by nonsocial work disciplines within academic settings, as well as community or church groups. Further, its ideals—human dignity, participation, nondiscrimination, transparency, and accountability (Androff, 2015)—are in line with today's social movements. Organizations interested in working globally could integrate this framework, following its guidance toward the development of practices that are ethical, collaborative, and reflective of shared humanity. Further, developing some uniformity in general "service practices" across providers would allow for meaningful comparisons and more diligent monitoring.

Social workers and social work educators could play an important role in the promulgation of this framework. Community members, clergy, and academics and students from diverse disciplines will be seeking information related to service trip leadership. Social workers are well equipped to provide training to leaders and participants alike. Business and organizations that contract with groups interested in service, acting as the liaison, would also benefit from such training, which they could then pass along to individuals on the trips they organize.

Elucidating the Model

The human rights-based perspective has only recently (2015) been embraced as a social work competency in our educational policies. Efforts to develop and articulate the vision supported by this framework should continue. It seems that the adoption of a human rights-based perspective is ipso facto a "result" and that perspective becomes a long-term outcome rather than a framework that illuminates clear steps and objectives. Certainly, diverse settings, diverse "helpers," and communities may make it impossible for us to develop a model that can be uniformly "applied," with clear and consistent steps. However, a flexible heuristic that includes guideposts that signal progress toward freedom for *all* members of a community should be within our reach.

CSWE provides some articulation of the framework's components. As noted above, CSWE indicates that the equal distribution of social goods and the protection of civil, political, environmental, economic, and cultural human rights are requisite conditions of a human rights approach to social work practice. Perhaps these types of justice can be viewed as building blocks or steps toward the pursuit of human justice and the protection of human rights.

The invocation of "steps" is used cautiously here. Ladder metaphors have dominated most helping professions, reducing development, for example, to a linear process with one beginning and one end. We might conceptualize the pursuit of justice as a lattice rather than a ladder. A lattice structure implies continued growth and development. It allows for movement laterally, diagonally, up, and down. Movements are effected by the structures around them. However, movement can be blocked. Movement on a lattice implies multiple paths "around" (acknowledging both diversity and difference in strategy) and suggests that there are many beginnings, ends, and paths toward an outcome. We might even imagine a circular or spherical lattice pattern, in which the connected circles reflect different types of justice, connected by multiple paths, leading toward human rights (visually situated at the circle's perimeter). Emanating from the hub of each sphere or type of justice might be indicators or objectives, formulated as questions. For economic justice: What is the minimum wage in the community you are "helping?" Are there opportunities for a living wage? Are all economic sectors viable and therefore accessible to citizens with different levels and types of training?

Regarding environmental justice: Where are dumping sites in this community? Are they concentrated in poorer neighborhoods? Is there access to clean water for all community members? Clarifying steps and strategies that move communities closer to justice and therefore the satisfaction of their human needs and protection of their human rights would allow us to respond effectively to the EPAS requirement that we diffuse our social work curricula with Competencies 2 and 3. This clarification might also provide changemakers with a map, strategy, and measurable objectives that facilitate our communities' journeys toward inclusion, equity, and well-being.

Summary

As social workers, our dedication to helping others has remained, but, over the years, our strategies for "helping" have not kept pace with the reality that well-intended efforts can quite easily fall short, be derailed by mission creep, or simply be poorly informed. Further, the social work profession is rooted in advocacy, social justice, and human rights. Short-term trips abroad have become a valued method of educating social work students while aligning with the mission and ethics of our profession. However, the human rights-based perspective is no less relevant to domestic service opportunities. We offer the human rights-based approach as a strategy that aligns with ideals of social work education, serves the higher objective of social justice, and preserves professional integrity. Moving from the field and back into the classroom, the human rights-based perspective has added utility.

Exercises

1. Recall service trips in which you have participated. Could they have benefitted from a clearer articulation of a framework, such as the human rights-based approach? If you had followed this framework, how would the trip have differed?
2. If you are an educator, how might the courses you teach change if you used the human rights-based approach to shape content? How might this framework change your pedagogy?

3. How might the profession of social work contribute to the promulgation of a human rights-based framework across different academic disciplines and different types of service groups?

References

Androff, D. (2015). *Practicing rights: Human rights-based approaches to social work practice*. https://doi.org/10.4324/9781315885483

CSWE. (2015). https://www.cswe.org/Accreditation/Standards-and-policies/2015-EPAS.

Hurd, E. (1998). Strengths-based teaching in social work. *Journal of Baccalaureate Social Work, 3*(2), 51–65.

Kahn, J., & Holody, R. (2009). WAC: A strengths-based approach to student learning. *Journal of Baccalaureate Social Work, 14*(1), 83–94.

Rice, K., & Girvin, H. (2010). Using a strengths-based perspective to change perceptions: An exploratory study. *Journal of Baccalaureate Social Work, 15*(2), 1–16.

Toros, K. (2019). Undergraduate students' perception of their own strengths and weaknesses as potential social workers. *Journal of Social Work Practice, 33*, 81–93.

Index

K. Rice, H. Girvin, *Human Rights-Based Approach to Short-Term Study Abroad*, SpringerBriefs in Rights-Based Approaches to Social Work,
https://doi.org/10.1007/978-3-030-87421-6

The manufacturer's authorised representative in the EU is Springer Nature Customer Service Centre GmbH, Europaplatz 3, 69115 Heidelberg, Germany. If you have any concerns regarding our products, please contact ProductSafety@springernature.com

Printed and bound by CPI Group (UK) Ltd, Croydon, CR0 4YY
30/09/2026
02225467-0003